Christmas in the Maritimes

A Treasury of Stories and Memories

NIMBUS
PUBLISHING

Edited by Elaine Ingalls Hogg

Nimbus Publishing Limited
PO Box 9166
Halifax, NS   B3K 5M8
(902) 455-4286

Printed and bound in Canada

Interior design: Kathy Kaulbach, Touchstone Design House

Inside cover art: Michael Oulton

"Christmas Rites" by Beth Powning extracted from *Edge Seasons* by Beth
Powning. Copyright © 2005 Powning Designs Limited. Reprinted by
permission of Knopf Canada.

Library and Archives Canada Cataloguing in Publication

Christmas in the Maritimes : a treasury of stories and
memories / edited by Elaine Ingalls Hogg.
ISBN 1-55109-594-7

1. Christmas—Atlantic Provinces. I. Hogg, Elaine Ingalls

GT4985.15.C567 2006   394.2663'09715   C2006-905120-8

Canada   The Canada Council | Le Conseil des Arts
          for the Arts | du Canada

We acknowledge the financial support of the Government of Canada
through the Book Publishing Industry Development Program (BPIDP)
and the Canada Council, and of the Province of Nova Scotia through
the Department of Tourism, Culture and Heritage for our publishing
activities.

Table of Contents

Christmas Toys and Santa Claus ... 75

Christmas Miracles and Gifts ... 103

Contributors ... 140

Introduction

WHEN CANADAEAST.COM EXTENDED an invitation for Maritimers to contribute their memories of "Christmas in the Maritimes," the stories poured in. Many recalled how an otherwise bleak Christmas was turned around by a thoughtful gift from a neighbour or a local charity, while others shared their family's unique tradition or special memories from childhood. Several stories arrived on the topic of seeing Santa and many more on selecting or decorating the family tree; one I particularly enjoyed was the story of the family that woke up early Christmas morning and discovered two pyjama-clad youngsters and their dog eating the freshly strung popcorn from their tree.

Because of the interest shown in this subject and the wide variety of stories submitted, the website Canadaeast.com and Nimbus Publishing decided to work together to bring these stories to a wider audience. As editor/compiler, I expanded the search range by putting out a call for submissions through the writers' federations and various contact lists.

Once again, the response was overwhelming. Everyone seemed to have a Christmas tale to tell.

Contributors told stories of participating in seasonal concerts, attending parties and family gatherings, and coming home for Christmas. Others shared memories of their first glimpse of Santa or attending a church service on Christmas Eve. Each story I received painted a picture of how we celebrate Christmas here in the Maritimes, so making a final selection was indeed difficult. The quality of the writing was taken into consideration, as was making certain each province was represented and that there was a balance of stories in each section; the most important factor, however, was certainly the emotional impact of the story.

Whether the memory was from a Christmas long ago or from a celebration more recent, collectively the stories speak of the significance and importance of this season in the hearts of Maritimers everywhere. This book tells of the importance of being together with family members, and the length we Maritimers are prepared to travel in order to make it home for the holidays. The anthology is an attempt to record a few of the things that make a Maritime Christmas special. It is my hope these tales and traditions will be instrumental in inspiring readers to continue the tradition of sharing their own tales with family, friends, and neighbours and to preserve them for future generations.

Elaine Ingalls Hogg

Christmas Traditions

"I have to make my grandmother's fruitcake," my friend said shortly after Thanksgiving last year. "Even though we only eat a small piece, it just wouldn't be Christmas without it." Personally, I'm not a baker but even I have one or two recipes that I try to make when I know the family is coming home over the holidays. It seems whether baking a favourite treat, writing cards, selecting a tree, or hanging a special ornament, most Maritimers have one tradition that leaps to mind when we mention the word "Christmas."

Perhaps the traditions followed most closely are the ones connected to Christmas Eve. Some folks make a last trip to the mall to watch the harried last-minute shoppers scurry about. Others are busy making food for the family's holiday feast either later that evening or the next day. In our family, we squirrel away in separate rooms in the house and wrap our presents. Then late at night when the lights are so low that we can't guess what is in the packages already arranged under its boughs, we'll tiptoe out to the tree and place gifts in neat piles to be opened early the next morning.

Attending a Christmas Eve church service is an oft-repeated memory for many Maritimers. Children were warned to behave during the service, and to assure this good behaviour, they were bribed either with the promise of being allowed to open one gift before bed or with the threat of Santa not coming if they were naughty.

Perhaps the best traditions involve family gatherings, remembering others with acts of kindness, and the fabulous stories that bind hearts together in the years when the children can no longer come home for Christmas.

Proof of the Pudding

JOYCE GERO

CURLED ON THE WINDOW SEAT in the upstairs hall, I slowly turned the pages of a new book, oblivious to freezing temperatures on the other side of the frost-swirled glass. Shiny white skates pressed against my hip, their new-leather smell mingling with kitchen aromas of roast turkey, dressing, and spicy carrot pudding. On the floor lay a bulging, oddly misshapen ribbed fawn stocking. As I read, my hand frequently crept inside, fingers wriggling past apples, oranges, and peanuts to search the toes for the candies I devoured along with the adventures of *The Bobbsey Twins at the Seashore*.

In the aftermath of Christmas gift exchange, the house was rich with silence, broken only by the occasional clatter of a pot lid or thud of a cupboard door, comfortable sounds of Mom preparing a proper noontime feast. Despite her warnings, my older brothers and sisters, as ready as I to spoil their appetites with unaccustomed treats, had also retired with their stockings to favourite nooks. For a family of avid readers, books were the most treasured of gifts, and this was a day for reading. A week of holidays stretched before us with plenty of time to break in new skates and sleds.

While we youngsters were absorbed in our books, Dad, too, was taking advantage of a rare opportunity for leisure. With my brothers' help, he'd finished the morning milking and given the cows their Christmas gift of an extra forkful of hay. On this day, the endless chores that normally occupied a farmer's time from before dawn to well beyond dusk could wait, and Dad lay snoring open-mouthed on the kitchen couch.

Meanwhile, Mom was concentrating on cooking the perfect holiday dinner for unappreciative children rapidly filling their bellies with chocolates, chicken bones, and barley toys. Unlike the rest of us, hers was a day filled with work, work, and more work. Besides the mundane morning tasks of straining and scalding raw milk, cooking breakfast, and making beds, she'd had a houseful of impatient, excited children to contend with on a day that had begun long before daybreak with a thirty-pound turkey waiting to be stuffed.

The night before, from a galvanised tub propped on two chairs in front of the old woodstove, I'd watched Mom wrestle the huge bird into a heavy white-speckled roasting pan. Cranberries were washed and sorted, cold potatoes brought out of the refrigerator and cubed for dressing. Tears streaming down her face, she'd supervised the bath ritual, normally reserved for Saturday nights, pausing to rinse the smell of chopped onions from her hands before wrapping me in a huge fluffy towel, toasty warm from a line hung above the stove.

Later, as we kids hung icicles, one by one, new strands glistening beside tarnished tinsel gleaned from last year's tree, Mom could be heard in the kitchen, grating carrots and chopping currants for her rich, spicy pudding, the traditional ending to our festive meal.

Hours later, the turkey golden brown and sizzling in the oven and a pudding-filled coffee can tightly sealed with aluminium foil steaming in a pan of boiling water on top of the range, her efforts were about to be rewarded.

"Time to set the table!"

I slid off the window seat, smoothed the crumpled pleats in my new tartan skirt, and trudged downstairs, one palm sliding along the polished rail, my eyes still riveted on the pages of the book clutched in my other hand. Reluctantly, I set *The Bobbsey Twins* aside and slipped into the dining room, where my sisters had already gathered.

The table, extended by several leaves, was hung with a glistening white lace cloth, company china, silverware, and crystal goblets waiting in stacks and clusters. It was our job to arrange place settings, set out dishes of pickles and cranberries, and pour water and juice. I was about to set a basket of rolls on the table when it happened.

Bang!

The sudden report sent me racing back to the kitchen, my sisters at my heels. Moments later, the boys appeared in the doorway to find Mom gaping in astonished dismay, her normally immaculate room spattered in golden brown. Her wonderful dessert had exploded, and pudding was everywhere! On the couch, Dad had dreamt peacefully on while the hot, spicy mixture rained down on him. We watched as, still sleeping, he began plucking bits from his shirt and popping them in his mouth.

Dad may have wished otherwise, but the "pudding incident" was never forgotten. Every Christmas, we teased him mercilessly about visions of sugar plums dancing in his head, and years later, when the story was passed on to his grandchildren, he was still grumpily insisting he'd awakened the instant the pudding exploded.

In the years following, mince and apple pie became our standard Christmas desserts, for Mom flatly refused to make the pudding again—a sorrowful ending for a family tradition, and the fabulous beginning of a family legend.

My Christmas Plans

TOM SHEPPARD

I BELIEVE THAT IN THIS YEAR of 1906 I'll get the wife a four-piece glass tea set, on sale for twenty-nine cents at George Banks's store in the village. She hinted to me that they had something she wanted, and the only other thing I saw her looking at in the store was a fur coat. Banks's ads say that some of the things they have there will make you laugh until you cry, but I laughed at the thought anyone would buy his wife a fur coat and cried when I saw the price.

The wife wanted to do her Christmas shopping up in Middleton. She has such itchy feet. She has never been to Middleton and begged to be allowed to go, saying she would take her sister along as a chaperone. She got out the train schedules and pointed out that she could take the Halifax and Southwestern from the Caledonia station at 7:40 in the morning, be in New Germany by nine, then change to the train to Middleton.

I doubted that would give her enough time to feed the chickens, get my breakfast on the table and have the children dressed and filled with porridge before going off to school. I said, "No," and reminded her that she always said, "If they don't have it down at the N. F. Douglas general store, you don't need it."

I would have thought she would have been satisfied when, only two years ago, I took her to Liverpool to shop. I had read in the newspaper that the packets *Daisy Vaughn* and *Harry B* were coming into the harbour from Halifax, laden with Christmas goods, after being delayed by inclement weather. The wife still has the ad from Mulhall's store saying that the packets were bringing them seventy-five boxes of raisins, five cases of currants, five thousand oranges, a half ton of figs, a whole ton of confectionery, ten kegs of choice grapes, twenty barrels of apples, nuts, dates and two barrels of cranberries.

George McLearn's store had Acme skates, sleds and crokinole games, and Miss Mollin's Millinery Store, opposite Court Street, had what the sign called dainty wares for dainty ladies. The wife winked at me and pointed at its door, but I asked who on earth we knew who was dainty. In fact, I had my mind set on a new Bissell carpet sweeper for her. "They raise no dust and make sweeping a delight," but she gave me a cold look when I stopped to inspect one. McLearn's ads also say the hardworking wife and mother would appreciate an Eze Wringer, which would go on the washtub, but the wife is strange in that she doesn't consider practical things to be gifts. So, I settled for some soap, a little mirror, and some perfume (the twenty-five cent kind, not the stuff that sells for ninety cents).

I remember on the way back we stopped at the Nathan Hammett Photographic Rooms, on Bridge Street. The wife wanted her picture taken to give to her mother. Hammett asked me if

A Bright and Happy Christmas.

I could make her smile, so I told her to give us a little whinny. She glared at me just as the powder flashed, and I told her that the picture would end up making the dog bark. As it turned out, Hammett made another one.

It is nothing short of amazing how much difference a couple of years will make. That year, to get to Liverpool, we had to take the mare and wagon. This year, now that the railroad has come to Liverpool, we can take the train from Caledonia across to New Germany, catch the Blueberry Express down to Bridgewater and then board the Halifax to Liverpool train. I heard one train came in to Liverpool the other day with eleven cars of freight, a baggage car and a passenger car. Mind you, folks here in the village are tickled that they had the train two whole years ahead of Liverpool.

I haven't decided on what to get the children yet. I might give the boy my old Winchester twelve-gauge now that I have the new Ithaca hammerless. The oldest girl has been grumbling to her mother over the chores I have given her, so I might get her some of those "Pink Pills for Pale People," said to be among the wonders of modern medicine. The newspapers say many girls her age go pale and weak, and you don't dare take the chance, as there is too much to be done on the home place. The ads say that Dr. Williams's Pink Pills will actually make new blood with every dose, stopping a young girl from wasting away. When I told the wife I had the perfect gift, and what it was, she gave me a peculiar look and said it had nothing to do with me. Well, enough of these challenges to my authority. I'll get them anyway, and the girl had better be grateful.

I saw in the paper that you can make picture frames from common gas pipe. I might make one of those, and put in it that portrait of myself. I could give that to the youngest girl, for her wall. Or, you can make a doorstop from a cobblestone painted with lampblack and household ammonia. She could use that to keep her bedroom door shut, and end her complaining about people barging in all the time.

Christmas Eve is only a short time away. I'm looking forward to it. I generally settle back with a glass or two of hard cider and watch the wife and children decorate the tree. As the evening wears on, the decorations go up, and the oil lamps cast their light, the wife brings in cookies with warm sweet cider for the children. A kind of mellowness settles over the room.

A Lick a Day

DEIRDRE KESSLER

(From *A Prince Edward Island Christmas: Nowadays and Long Ago*, 2004, and *A Century on Spring Street*).

THOUGH CATALOGUES AND STORES advertised and displayed many handsome gifts and toys, most Prince Edward Islanders remember the gifts of Christmases past as being very humble ones. Children would hang up a stocking for St. Nicholas and be delighted on Christmas morning to find an apple or an orange, a bit of hard candy, and perhaps a small handmade toy.

In 2001, James, a grade seven student at St. Teresa School, interviewed Mabel, a senior citizen of the Baldwin's Road area near the school, about the Christmas traditions of her childhood in the 1920s. Mabel said she got a train-shaped candy in her stocking on Christmas morning when she was a little girl, "but I only had a lick a day until it was gone, and that was near Easter."

In contrast with the paucity of gifts Mabel received, in 1901 six-year-old Wanda Lefurgey Wyatt of Summerside practised joined-up writing in a letter to her grandmother, Randal Spencer Wyatt of Charlottetown, to describe the presents she had received that Christmas.

Summerside
Dec. 29th 1901
Dear Grandma,
We hope you spent a very Happy Xmas. Mama had the Xmas
dinner we ate so much couldn't take any tea. Santi Claus was very
good to me I got a doll chair and doll to fit it a Painting and crayon
book a box of Puzzles, spelling board a lovely gold ring from Uncle
Al a box of kisses and a box of paper I am now Writing on. We are
practising for a concert in the Guild room tomorrow night. With love
to Dohathy and baby.
Your loving Wanda

Robbie Robertson of Kingsboro, born in 1904, told Dutch
Thompson about his Christmas memories in an interview
in 1995: "In the Christmas stocking we got an apple, an
orange, and raisins. No toys. I had thirteen brothers and
sisters. Mother died when I was thirteen years old." And
Nina Brown, born in 1902, told Dutch, "Our house was like
Mrs. Hubbard's cupboard. In our stocking we got an orange,
candy, and perhaps a package of gum." Jeannette MacVittie
MacDonald, born in 1903 and raised in Westmoreland, near
Crapaud, said: "If we got a sucker, an all-day sucker, we
were doing pretty good. Or we'd get one of those candies
you can see through, perhaps in the shape of a lion or a bear.
I wouldn't even bother to hang up a stocking. My brother
would hang up his schoolbag on the closet door, and sometimes he'd get something, an orange or something."

Christmas Singing Traditions in Nova Scotia

CLARY CROFT

(adapted from *Celebrate: The History and Folklore of Holidays in Nova Scotia*)

WE NOVA SCOTIANS have a great reputation as singers and Christmas gives us a chance to shine. And one was never limited to the standard holiday repertoire. At Chezzetcook, the men would sit opposite one another at a table holding a handkerchief between them and sing the old traditional ballads.

For some Nova Scotians, carols were reserved for church. Christmas gatherings were often seen as a time for secular music and dancing. At Port la Tour, they played harmonicas, tambourines, and violins. At Mahone Bay, an auto harp and triangle were added to these instruments. Music and step-dancing was often so lively that the telephone lines at the party were left open for the neighbours to enjoy. At Chezzetcook, the people danced plain sets, lancers, polkas and waltzes. At Bear River, Mi'kmaq informants told the Maritimes' great folklore collector, Helen Creighton, that they enjoyed Christmas celebrations by dancing old-fashioned eights and end with war dances. Lawson Innes of Peggy's Cove told her: "We always had two or three fiddles and would sing by-times, and occasionally would make a song up. Rube Dobbin could do that; he was our santa claw. We made our own decorations and children hung their stockings all round the chimney corner, oh my, mighty yes!"

Not only did we enjoy our music at home—we frequently shared it with others in the province and even on a national scale. From the *South Shore Record* (Mahone Bay) for 16 December 1937 comes the following announcement: "The Lunenburg Glee Club has again brought honour to its native town, as it has been chosen to take part in the

National broadcast on Christmas Day." The broadcast featured twenty-five singers and an accompanist playing the pipe organ. Most fittingly for Lunenburg, the performance included two songs in German: "Silent Night" and "O Tannenbaum," as well as "O Little Town of Bethlehem."

Christmas music broadcasts have also become a traditional part of African Nova Scotian culture. In 1931, children from the *Nova Scotia Home for Coloured Children* were taken to radio station CHNS in Halifax. There they performed live in efforts to raise funds for the institution. Their repertoire included some traditional African Nova Scotian folk songs, but was made up primarily of standard Christmas tunes. The broadcast proved so popular that soon the show was being transmitted live from the home and had the addition of adult performers, all helping to raise funds for the home. The fund-raising broadcasts continue today, only now the medium used is television.

Radio station CHNS also gave Nova Scotians in Halifax and the surrounding area live Christmas broadcasts from the Simpson's department store. In the early years, these included live orchestras and professional singers, while later on the music was often provided by Dick Fry at the Hammond organ with the store employees singing. It was a regular holiday tradition in my house to tune in and sing along with the Christmas songs, especially since the lyrics had been provided through the local newspaper. It was probably the biggest Christmas carol sing-a-long the province ever had!

My mother tells me I was singing almost before I could talk, so it was natural for me to be involved in every Christmas pageant and concert at Sunday school and grade school. However, one of my first public appearances almost ended in disaster and may have squelched a budding career. I would have been around five years old and my friend, Linda Scott, a couple of years older. We were to sing a duet at our Christmas concert which was held in the basement of the Presbyterian Church in

Sherbrooke. I'm sure we were dressed to the nines. We took our places, the piano accompaniment began and we both started giggling. I don't remember if we even got through the song—or what the song was for that matter. I have some kind of residual memory of being taken off the stage. I know that I've blocked that part of the scenario from my mind and poor Linda probably made the decision then and there to end a promising career as an entertainer. In later years, I was always a featured performer at Christmas concerts, but it's nice to remember how even the mighty can be reduced to social ridicule. And that, I'm sure, is just one of thousands of disaster stories from Christmas concert lore.

How many juvenile elocutionists were letter-perfect before the big event only to need repeated prompting from a teacher in the wings once the event was underway? How many understudies have had to step in and raise the letter X in the M-E-R-R-Y X-M-A-S message when the original child came down with the holiday flu? How many little boys performed with the indignity of an unzipped fly? How many little girls had their personal appearances drastically altered by an unsuccessful home permanent the night before their major debut? Who knows, maybe Christmas concerts are a subliminal way to discourage children from pursuing a life on the stage.

But what I hope most children remember about their Christmas concerts is the fun and excitement of rehearsal; of peeking through the curtain to find mom and dad sitting proudly in the front row; of delivering their four-line Christmas verse in syllables that even the gap left by two missing front teeth couldn't blur; and of singing much-loved Christmas songs, even if the music teacher told them, "Since you're a crow, dear, and will never be a bluebird—just mouth the words!" Sorry, not tonight lady! This was one time you could lift your tuneless little voice and join the angelic chorus. I always felt sorry for those kids and was glad when I heard them singing next to me. After all, singing along with Christmas songs is one of life's great pleasures.

Don't Worry, We'll Have Christmas Tomorrow

MONICA GRAHAM

WE MADE A RULE early in our marriage that we would spend Christmas at home, and we followed it for twenty-five years—until the season of "The Big Blow."

At 4:00 A.M. Christmas Day, a fierce wind knocked out power and telephone lines in our half of the county, and woke me up. I switched off the TV, the fridge, and the computer so they wouldn't be damaged by returning electricity, and fell back into bed.

An hour later, the power came back on, but it burned out, with a white and blue flash, half the bulbs I switched on. The other half glowed eerily red. Weird! Time to consult my husband.

"Don't worry," was his semi-snored response. "The repair crews will be out soon."

"On Christmas morning? They probably have families, too," I said. He snored on.

Why were the lights acting so weirdly? Would the house catch fire? I wanted to know.

"Go back to bed," said my husband. "There's nothing you can do."

Against my better judgment, I complied. Any other Christmas, everyone would have been up for hours by now. But there I was on watch all alone, listening for sparks.

When dawn cracked, I peered out the window towards the line of power poles extending to the highway, one hundred metres away. I couldn't see a thing for the swaying branches and the dim light. "I'm going to call the power company," I told Fred, who didn't wake up. The phone line was dead.

"I'm going to Mary Lou's to call the power company," I told Fred. He didn't budge. Mary Lou lives next door, half a kilometre away.

Pulling on outdoor clothes over my pyjamas, I drove out the lane and immediately discovered the problem. A giant spruce lay splintered over both lines, which dangled just high enough off the ground for me to drive underneath. The wind see-sawed the trunk back and forth over the power cable, showering intermittent sparks.

Debating whether to go back in the house and wake everyone up in case of fire, or alert the power company before someone was hurt, I opted for the latter. It should only take a few minutes, I reasoned.

Mary Lou's family was halfway through the gifts piled under a Christmas tree that glowed with electric light. Unfortunately, their phone was out of order.

"Try the highway shed," advised her husband. "There's always someone there, and he'll be able to contact the power company directly."

I tore off to the highway department, twelve kilometres away, but it was locked up solidly. Rain began slanting down the neck of my jacket, and I wondered what to do next.

Shivering under the eave, I spied a family coming out of their house across the road. They were leaving to spend Christmas Day with relatives, they said, but they could delay their departure while I called the power company.

The line was busy, busy, busy. I finally called the Mounties, and persuaded them it was a dangerous situation. They promised to call the repair crews right away.

Back at home, Fred was still asleep. I shook him awake to ask if I should pull the main power switch.

"Why?" he asked.

I told him.

"Why didn't you tell me before?" he said. "The house could have caught fire."

He pulled the main himself, and then unearthed our camping stove and used a bicycle pump to draw water from the well for coffee. By then, our almost-grown-up kids were awake, clamouring for the Christmas morning routine.

It was a forgettable Christmas brunch. Instead of a cosy, leisurely breakfast of waffles, sausages, and maple syrup, we ate greasy camp-fried eggs—the only bird cooked at our house that day. Candlelight failed to banish the greyness, and our electrically heated house began to chill. The usual gift opening warmed our hearts, but not our feet.

"What about the turkey?" asked our practical oldest son.

Fred announced we'd cook it and the vegetables at our daughter's apartment in town, fifteen kilometres away.

Without a telephone, we couldn't call to warn her. Our oldest son drove away with the turkey, and Fred and I and our youngest son followed with the vegetables.

Almost there, we met our oldest boy coming the other way. He waved, we waved back, and Fred refused to stop. "He going to his girlfriend's," he said.

Wrong. At our daughter's we discovered her electricity had also failed. She'd sent her brother home to cook the turkey on our gas barbecue.

We all piled in the car to follow him, but again met our son coming toward us. This time Fred stopped. "We're out of propane," the boy said.

Our son-in-law took our son to fetch the full tank at their apartment, while the rest of us continued home. The downed wires were still down, so Fred started a fire in the wood stove with balled-up Christmas wrapping.

Our son and son-in-law arrived with the propane tank. "The power's on in town," they said. "Let's go."

Family and food piled into town, but had exactly 20 minutes of electricity before it went dark and silent. "That's it," Fred said, standing up and putting on his coat. "I'm going home and I'm going back to bed. We'll have Christmas to-morrow."

Our daughter and son-in-law decided to visit his parents in Halifax, two hours away.

Good idea. We went home, shoved the turkey in the fridge, and did a safety check.

"Get in the car," bawled Fred, and we drove off to my brother's in Halifax.

We met the power truck on the way, but we never looked back. We had a lovely Christmas in Halifax, and when we got home on Boxing Day the power was on and the phone worked.

A New Brunswick Christmas— My Parents' Christmas Memories

ELAINE INGALLS HOGG

AS THE DECEMBER DAYS GOT SHORTER, excitement mounted in the Ingalls family home. Christmas was coming. In every house along "the Point"—the name we called our neighbourhood (Ingalls Head, Grand Manan, New Brunswick)—the mothers were busy baking for Christmas. Grandma Ingalls made butterscotch and mincemeat pies. Aunt Ruth made a special gumdrop cake with red, green and yellow gumdrops all through it and most of the homes made fruit-cakes. My mother made "War Cakes." These dark spice cakes made with dried raisins were a tradition passed along on her side of the family as raisins were the only fruit her family could buy during the war. Once the cakes were cooked, my brother Perry and I decorated them with white icing and coloured cake decorations. Together we marked off the days until Christmas on the kitchen calendar.

During the long evenings, the family sat around the kitchen table and listened to the announcer on the small brown radio read the fisherman's news and weather. After the supper dishes were washed and put away, we begged our parents to tell us "Once Upon a Time Stories" about life when they were children.

When asked about his Christmas memories, Dad cleared his throat and said, "In my parents' home, the job of looking for the perfect Christmas tree fell to my older brother, Henry. Sometimes he disappeared for the whole day and went tramping in the woods looking for the right tree. More than once he came home with no tree at all. Ma wanted the most perfect tree in the forest. She wanted to be proud of how it looked in the living room when the neighbours did their Christmas calling. Sometimes Henry came home so tired he could hardly walk the last few steps into the house. He would take his coat and boots off in the porch then enter the warm kitchen. For a long time he sat at the kitchen table near the warmth of the black stove and sipped mugs of hot tea to get warmed up after his tramp in the woods. Meanwhile Ma worked at making supper in the small pantry just off the kitchen and Henry would tell her of the different trees he saw and why he didn't choose them. 'One was perfect on the good side but it had a couple of branches missing,' he'd tell her or 'I saw a perfect one when I first went in to the woods but I left it to see if there was a better one and when I came back someone else had cut it down. But I'll get one tomorrow,' he said reassuringly.

"In those days (1920s), Ma and Pa went to Eastport by boat at the beginning of December and they returned home with many packages but we were never allowed to peek inside. After one of those trips my brother Hayward and I received matching sheepskin jackets and hip rubber boots under the tree on Christmas morning. Two other special gifts I received on different Christmas mornings were a toy horse rigged and harnessed to a tiny cart and a little red wagon with real tires that I had to share with Hayward."

When dad was finished it was my mother's turn to tell
her stories. "When I was little," she began, "the excitement
started with the arrival of the Eaton's and Sears Roebuck
catalogues. As the day approached, my Aunt Lila began the
cleaning," said Mom. "We had to clean every nook and
cranny. There couldn't be even a smooch of dust or a cob-
web anywhere. We cleaned the back of the flour containers
and under the cupboards. The curtains were washed and
the house was polished from top to bottom. Aunt Lila said
Santa would think we were slovenly if we didn't get rid of
all the dirt.

"The preparation at school was just as exciting as we
practised for the school Christmas program. All the children in my class practised their parts in the play or their
songs for the choir. The classroom blackboards were
washed clean and then decorated with Christmas pictures.
We made paper decorations like paper lanterns or long paper chains and hung them in the classroom. On the night
of the Christmas concert, Santa came down through a
chimney. We didn't have a real chimney in our school. In
the winter, the classroom was heated by a little black stove
that sat in the middle of the room. But we all thought we
needed a chimney for Santa, so the older boys built one
from old bits of wood for the night of the concert.

"I can still remember some of the verses that my class-
mates recited in the concert:

Old Thanta Claus is short and fat
So I've been told by ma.
I thaw him, he's tall and thin
And looks just like my Pa!

"My parents raised geese to sell at this time of year. Unfortunately, the geese seemed to sense that Christmas dinner was being planned and they went wild. In the Shepherd home, getting geese ready for sale was as much a part
of Christmas as finding the tree. I can remember feathers
everywhere. They drifted all through the house. Feath-

ers, feathers, feathers! They stuck to clothes, furniture, and curtains but most embarrassing was how they stuck to our Sunday clothes. The whole neighbourhood soon knew that it was goose-plucking time in the Shepherd household."

"Christmas Eve," mother continued, "began with chores that the children completed before the celebrations could begin. There were barn chores, the wood box was filled, supper dishes were washed and the water pails were filled for the morning. After chores, the family gathered in the living room around the cosy stove. We watched the glow of the flickering flames from the coal fire as it reflected on the icy windowpanes. The family gathered in a circle within the warmth of the little stove. The candles on the tree were lit and these added their magic to the quiet glow in the room."

A Cape Breton Christmas

SANDRA BOUTQUIN

I DON'T OFTEN WAX NOSTALGIC; I'm usually very much with the times, but I know if I could have a wish granted, spending Christmas in the Maritimes would be at the top of my list.

When I was growing up in North Sydney, I don't ever remember having what's euphemistically known as a "green Christmas." All the Christmases that I remember were extremely white. I remember blizzards, hip-deep snow, gale force winds and not being able to get the door open. My brother had to wade through the snow to bring in coal and kindling for the kitchen stove.

Being the hardy souls that we were, the weather never stopped my family from getting together at Christmas to celebrate. Aunt Nina with my cousin Joan, Aunt Pearl, Aunt Jessie with my two cousins, Raymond and David, and my grandmother—who we called Nan—would all come from Sydney on Christmas Day for dinner. For those of you not in the know, dinner was at noon. We had breakfast, dinner and supper. Dinner in the evening was for movie stars and the like.

My family's roots are in Newfoundland. When Newfoundland became part of Canada, courtesy of Joey Smallwood, we were the first ones on a boat to a better life in Nova Scotia. It was akin to leaving Ireland during the potato famine and immigrating to the New World. My mother was ecstatic, my father considerably less so.

With the Newfie influence, our Christmases took on a bit of a British flavour. My mother told my brother and me about the mummers in Newfoundland who would go around from house to house having a bit of a mug-up at each place. (Again, for those of you unfortunate enough not to come from the better part of the country, a mug-up is a lunch usually served in the evening.) By the end of the evening, the mummers were decidedly the worse for wear, what with the legendary Newfie hospitality. We pulled Christmas crackers, we wore the hats that were inside them and along with our turkey and stuffing, we had plum pudding with money and a button baked in it. If you got the button, you were the Old Maid. I used to hold my breath, hoping that I wouldn't have to endure the humiliation of finding that button in my portion.

At Park Street School, we had annual Christmas concerts. In a small town like North Sydney, this was one of the social events of the season, along with the pageant that Sunday School put on. I was a shepherd girl—I so wanted to be an angel. We were scrubbed to within an inch of our lives with Lifebuoy soap and decked out in our holiday finery. What a sight—the whole grade two class standing up together fervently singing "Oh Come All Ye Faithful."

Some of us could even sing in key.

From an early age, my brother and I were assigned to go out and cut down the Christmas tree. "Get a nice fir," my mother would tell us, "don't get a spruce, the needles fall off." We walked to the woods, not too far away, and usually fought over which tree we'd get. My brother always won and we'd drag it home, exhausted by the time we got there. We'd put the big old light strings on the tree, and remember the old lead icicles? We'd hang those on, neatly at first; as we got a bit tired, we'd just fling them. We weren't terribly concerned about lead poisoning back then.

It was a treat to go downtown to the old stone post office each day for the mail. I'd wait in line impatiently until I got to the wicket and asked if there was any mail for our family. If I was lucky, there'd be Christmas cards from far away friends and relatives. The Salvation Army Band was always on the corner by Thompson and Sutherland's—I loved the tambourine and the bass drum. If I had a nickel, I would put it in the red kettle for those less fortunate.

THE · NIGHT BEFORE · CHRISTMAS BY CLEMENT · C · MOORE · LLD ILLUSTRATED · BY ARTHUR · RACKHAM

My brother and I used to shop at Stedman's, the local five-and-ten. It had old wooden floors and dim lighting, but none of that could dull our excitement at having a whole dollar to spend on our mother's present and another dollar to spend on each other.

I was so excited on Christmas Eve that I could never get to sleep. I'd call out to my mother, "Did Santa come yet?" and she'd answer, "No, he won't come until after you go to sleep." Sleep just wouldn't come! In the morning, probably at the crack of dawn, I'd open my stocking—just an old stocking that my mother had knitted. In it would be an apple, an orange, some nuts, some hard candy and maybe a ball or some other small toy. Then I got to open my presents—there were only three or four, all wrapped in red and green tissue paper. The writing on the ones from Santa looked suspiciously familiar, but I still believed! I was thrilled if I got a doll and maybe a set of dishes. My brother usually got a Meccano set and one year he got cowboy guns on a gun belt. He was in heaven.

I never gave much thought to all the work my mother had to do to have a nice Christmas for us or how much it cost. Santa brought everything and, of course, my mother did all the cooking. That was the way it was supposed to be.

Christmas in the Maritimes when I was growing up was enchanting; it took forever to arrive and was gone before you knew it. It was all about family and friends and getting together to have a good time. It had very little to do with all of the glitz and glamour we are so used to today. I wish it could be like that again.

Memories of Christmases Past

DEVONNA EDWARDS

MEMORIES OF GROWING UP in the 1950s and '60s in Fairview, Nova Scotia, bring back wonderful recollections. As the holidays drew nearer, there wasn't much school work accomplished as we were all too busy making decorations. A bare Christmas tree stood in the corner of our classroom like Cinderella waiting for her ball gown.

The annual school Christmas concert added to our delight. In late November, the music teacher undertook the
task of preparing her little singers, actors, and musicians
to perform in front of a live audience. Our poor, suffering teacher—how her head and eardrums must have ached
with all the clatter and noise. But with patience and perseverance she shaped her pupils into dedicated entertainers.
The members of the band wore short, colourful caps and
a small pillbox-type hat that tied under the chin. Singers
belted out Christmas carols and for once it didn't matter
what colour bird you were, everyone got to sing. (A blue
bird meant you were a good singer, a yellow bird meant fair
and a red bird meant you were terrible.)

Students also acted in different plays. There was a bustle
of activities at this time, and on the night of the concert
everything came together. If there were any glitches, no
one seemed to mind. The auditorium was filled to capacity. A huge, wonderfully decorated Christmas tree stood at
one corner of the stage. Pupils wearing their very best attire
were seated in their classrooms, waiting for the teacher to
tell them, "It's show time!" Butterflies danced in their tum-
mies as the children walked single file to a narrow room
beside the stage. Finally, the curtains opened and there were
hundreds of faces looking back.

At home the excitement was unbearable. Mom spent days
making our house shine, and I remember the smell of John-
son's hard wax on the floors. Christmas cards arrived daily.
After school was out for the holidays, our letters were mailed
to Santa and we children began shopping for our parents.
Old Spice aftershave for Dad and Evening-In-Paris perfume
for Mom. Woolworth's at the Bayer's Road Shopping Centre was the popular shopping place for us children.

Early on Christmas Eve it was off to confession. On
the way home I remember the snow falling softly and
sparkling in the moonlight. The Christmas lights on the
houses looked so festive and everything seemed to be so

tranquil and hushed. Arriving home, the smell of spices filled the air and there was always a large bowl of fruit overflowing in the centre of the table. Clare candy and Pot of Gold chocolates were also stacked in dishes through the house—a real treat!

Our Christmas tree stood in the corner of the living room, but was not decorated until all the family arrived home to help. My dad worked on Christmas Eve at his pharmacy (O'Brien's Pharmacy on Dutch Village Road). He tried to close the store early but not before several calls were made to him from home, "Bring home more lights, we need more tinsel." When dad finally arrived home he put the star on top of the tree and then the decorating began. The tree was decorated in record time as there were so many helping hands.

Next, it was time to hang our stockings on the mantel, our longest sock of course. We hurried to put out Santa's cookies and milk, and then off to bed we went for the longest night of the year. Time and time again I told my siblings, "Go to sleep; Santa won't come if you're awake!" Struggling to keep our eyes closed, we were sure we heard Santa and his reindeer on the roof. Finally sleep would claim us only to awake at three or four in the morning to be told by dad, "Go back to sleep, Santa hasn't come yet!" Around 5:00 A.M. we crept down the stairs. Santa had arrived! The room was stacked full of toys in ten individual piles. Some of the gifts I remember are a beautiful ballerina doll, dishes and cut-out dolls.

My brother Nonnie (John) got a full Davy Crocket outfit and rifle. Brother Patty received a cowboy outfit with gun, holster, spurs, and a rocking horse. Brother Shaun's favourite gift was a Johnny Seven Gun—"It really could do seven things!" he still exclaims. Sister Colleen remembers her pink cardboard make-up table and chair. Prima, who was our New Year's Day baby, once thought that she got coal in her sock and howled loudly until our mom told her that she had the wrong sock, it was Dad's. Mom put a piece of coal in it as a joke! Sister Maureen just tried to find a small, quiet spot behind the tree to play with her new doll. Mike (Michelle) long remembered her doll too, mostly the smell of her brand-new Barbie. Holly was our Boxing Day baby. Mary Ellen's favourite memory was how special the Christmas tree looked in the moonlight. How we hated to leave our presents to go to Christmas Mass! Our parents had to remind us that it was Christ's birthday, and off we went.

The Light at Christmas

RUTH EDGETT

ON CHRISTMAS EVE in 1935, a mariner far out in St. George's Bay might see the steady red glow of the Pomquet Island light and take comfort that it meant safe harbour at Bayfield, should he need to make use of it. He would know that, until the mid-January ice brought an end to navigation in this part of northeastern Nova Scotia, the beacon would reach out every night from its square, white tower.

Attached to this tower in 1935 would be a house, and inside the house, six children ranging in age from fourteen years to eleven months. If it were, say, seven o'clock in the evening, they might be in the dining room with their parents, George and Ruth Millar, hanging stockings from the clock shelf. Every year at this time, the eight-day clock and its two kerosene lamp companions would be underscored by a jagged row of expectant socks. They would not be the store-bought kind with embroidered names or appliquéd Santa faces. These would be real, working socks, the kind a person might pull on before plunging feet into gum rubber boots and heading for the barn.

Christmas morning—before George had a chance to extinguish the tower light at dawn—the children would clamber downstairs. Once more in the dining room, they would find each woolen toe stretched bulbous by an orange, a rare and exotic fruit at the time, and every legging stuffed with Biblical shapes of barley sugar candy, which would be held in trust by their mother and paid out gradually. Each child would find within his or her own sock something special. It might be a small pull toy, a tin soldier, a painted doll or, for baby Barbara, a celluloid rattle.

After breakfast, the children could move to the parlour where George would have stoked the coal-fired pot-bellied stove, and where the tree would have been decorated some days earlier with pencil twists of coloured paper. From Santa, there might be Hardy Boys or Dave Dawson books for Malcolm and David and, perhaps, Nancy Drew adventures or more L. M. Montgomery novels for Thelma, Rosa, and Minna. There would be something for the parents, too. With their money earned picking summer potato bugs, the children would have bought, perhaps, a Wilf Carter record for George or a pretty pin cushion for Ruth. There would be useful articles of clothing from Grandpa and Grandma Mitchell. These new things might be enjoyed to the tune of Christmas carols played by Ruth on her pump organ, if time permitted.

In a household where neither time nor money was ever wasted, this would be a day of plenty. For breakfast, there would be potted head Ruth had carefully seasoned and pressed into its scallop-edged mould a month or so beforehand when George had slaughtered the pig. For the main meal, there would be a fully dressed chicken, which had been selected a day or two earlier from the yard. Garden vegetables would be brought up from the cellar, along with homemade gingersnaps, mincemeat pie, doughnuts, pudding, and a meticulously crafted fruitcake.

In many respects, Christmas for the Millars was much the same as it was for other families in Antigonish County. What made it different was not so much the ritual of the celebration, but the isolation of the celebrants. Far out in the large bay that separates the northern half of the Nova Scotia peninsula from the island of Cape Breton, the water would be deep and cold but not yet frozen over. In the southwestern corner, though, in the quarter-mile passage between tiny Pomquet Island and the Bayfield Harbour breakwater, the lolly would be just beginning to form. Until it turned to hard, honest ice there could be no access to the mainland either on foot or by boat.

For at least a month now, Thelma, Rosa and Malcolm would have conceded to worsening weather and reverted to education courtesy of their mother and the Nova Scotia Correspondence Study program. Although they'd been allowed to practice Christmas carols with their mainland schoolmates until they had to leave school in the fall, the annual Christmas concert itself was unattainable. Even a winter church service would be unlikely.

Still, Christmas was a time of excitement. Official preparations began in November. That was when George journeyed to the mainland post office and returned with a sack full of presents and that was when Ruth baked the Christmas cake. She would start early in the morning by nursing the wood-fired flame in the kitchen stove and assigning her daughters to cut up the candied fruit that went into the batter. When she was certain the oven had reached the perfect temperature, and when she could stand her wooden spoon in the middle of the bowl, Ruth would pour the mixture into a baking pan and slide it into the oven. While it cooked, the children would be sent outdoors, or made quiet indoors, lest they disturb its delicate rising.

Well before this, even, George would have selected the tree. On summer passes through the Pomquet Island woods, he would have been looking out for and marking the best one. Then, a week or so before the big day, the children would bundle up in their boots, coats and hats to follow their father into the bush where he would fell the tree and haul it home. This annual event was something George would not mention to his superiors at the Department of Marine and Fisheries. In order to preserve the island's "wooded" appearance, as described in the government's information for mariners, no tree on these twenty-five acres was to be cut. Even firewood came from the mainland.

With the exception of this Christmas secret, George observed his light-keeping duties religiously. As long as boats traversed St. George's Bay in winter, Pomquet Island's ruby light could be seen, giving anyone who sailed there an invitation to safe harbour and a passing hint of Christmas warmth.

The Runaway Horse

CLARICE POIRIER

WE HADN'T BEEN TO MIDNIGHT MASS for years, as we had nobody to look after the children. So the first year that we were in Traveller's Rest, we planned to go to midnight mass as our eldest daughter was old enough to look after the youngest ones, and they would all be in bed by the time we would leave anyway. When my husband's boss heard we were planning on going to midnight mass, he said, "Why don't you take the trotter and the light sleigh?" Now this was a very special horse and a very fancy sleigh. So we left at about 10:00 P.M. as we wanted to visit with my sister and her husband who lived in Summerside and were coming with us to midnight mass. I remember it was such a beautiful calm frosty night; we even had sleigh bells that made a lovely musical sound and a buffalo robe to put over our knees to keep us warm. I remember my husband saying,

"Well it sure won't take us long to get home."

When we arrived at my sister's, my husband and brother-in-law put the horse in a small shed. My husband, Edmund, also put a blanket over the horse and gave him some hay. The horse seemed very contented. Then we walked to church; we were just in time for mass.

After mass we walked back to my sister's, and when we arrived there, they made us go in for a cup of tea and a piece of pâté. Edmund checked the horse, but it was fine, so we all went in and had our pâté.

Then we had to leave for home, as by that time it was coming on morning. Well, when we got to the shed, low and behold, our horse was gone. I think the horse got nervous hearing us arrive back from church. My husband and brother-in-law walked around town, got in touch with the cops, but no one had seen the horse. The only solution left for us was to walk home. We thought if we took the railroad track, we would avoid all the traffic. Well, what a mistake that was, as that was the year we had an awful lot of snow. The snow banks were so very high on both sides of the tracks. All of a sudden we heard a train coming and all we could do was push ourselves into the soft snow on each side of the tracks. It was quite an experience when the train went whizzing by. I hope we never come that close to the Grim Reaper again.

We left the tracks at Traveller's Rest but we still had a couple of miles to walk to our house. When we got home, Edmund had to go and tell his boss about the horse, but when he got there, the horse was standing in front of the barn all covered in white foam.

I only had time to get my coat off when I heard our kids getting up. Their first words from upstairs were, "Momee, did Santa Clause come yet?" In those days, there was nothing under the tree before the children were all asleep. Well, I tell you it took some scrambling around trying to get things organized before they all came trooping downstairs.

Those were very happy days. We really miss our family and those good old days. To top it all off, I had seven extra people invited for Christmas dinner that night; that is, besides my own family! Oh, did our bed ever feel good that night.

We Don't Do Christmas!

GILLIAN

"IT'S LIKE GOING BACK TO THE FIFTIES."
"Family is important here."
"It's a slower pace."
"It's…different."
These were the comments from our friends, other refugees from Ontario, who'd made the leap in moving to Nova Scotia five, ten and even fifteen years earlier. Now it was our turn. We'd had a child late in life and had a strong urge to raise her in an atmosphere where kids still played ball hockey on the streets and you didn't need a palm pilot to organize their activities. For me, however, there was one looming issue…Christmas!

It's such an important season for Maritimers (they even publish books devoted to heartwarming Christmas stories) but, since my teens, I've hated it. I put my poor nuclear family through hell trying to redo the holiday in my minimalist image. One year instead of giving presents I wrote them a long poem—good Lord!

Time passed. I met Frank who had two small children. Since my family always ate the turkey at one o'clock in the afternoon and Frank's at around five, we could have Christmas dinner with both. Now, my side always had mashed potatoes and Brussels sprouts with the enormous turkey. Frank felt my side was a little too stuck in our ways and it was time to shake us up with something different so he said he would provide the vegetables, sweet potatoes and green peas. This alarming swing from tradition didn't faze my father who still put out the mashed potatoes and Brussels sprouts. After that meal and a suitable visit we went on to Frank's parents' where his mother had cooked an enormous turkey…accompanied by sweet potatoes and green peas. Driving back to our apartment I rolled down the window and left two identical Christmas dinners on the shoulder of the Queen Elizabeth Highway—never again!

Even once our daughter was born I had no trouble resisting the season. I'd heard a CBC radio program on the whole issue and remembered the commentator saying that Canadian families spend an average of twelve hundred dollars each year at Christmas. Bah, humbug. No sooner were the jack-o'-lanterns disposed of than flyers advertising "The Perfect Gift for Him" appeared in the mailbox and children were being told, "Only thirty more sleeps till Santa!" Thirty? Might as well be a hundred to a four-year-old. With this attitude, we three were well established as people who don't "do" Christmas. That's what we told our new friends in Wolfville, Nova Scotia.

"We don't do Christmas."

The response earned us some puzzled looks, but then we were weird enough—we'd driven three provinces in the tail end of a hurricane so we could put our daughter in a school without curriculum, plus Frank does Tai Chi in the driveway every morning. Nova Scotians are famously tolerant.

We resolutely did not buy any presents ourselves so I clenched my teeth when the first of the presents came to us. I said "thank you" and set it aside. Then one day we found a little gift bag hanging on the door handle for our daughter. I set that aside, too. These Nova Scotians just weren't getting it, we don't do Christmas. We'd formed a close friendship with a family up the street—our daughters play long and hard together on weekends and after school—surely they'd heard us when we'd said we don't do Christmas? Apparently not, as there was a gift bag from the parents and a gift bag for our daughter from the two girls.

Humbug!

What to do? I resolutely did not dash off to Zellers for a toy that would immediately break, as I might have done in Ontario. Once you start giving presents it's not long before you're putting on Santa earrings, going to cookie exchanges, and showing up at parties with a bottle of wine. Could an enormous turkey with sweet potatoes and green peas be far behind? No sir, I'd nip this thing in the bud and nip it early before it got out of hand. Next year they'd realize that we really…don't…do…Christmas.

Then we opened our presents. The first contained three different kinds of lovely homemade jam. The one that had been hanging on the doorknob held an ornament made of clay with our daughter's name on it—Risa—and a lump of clay for her to make of it what she would. Our neighbours had given us more jam and a jar of homemade green tomato relish so delicious that I spoon it into my mouth directly from the jar.

But the present that touches me most was the one from the little girls, the present I had dreaded, the one I had worried would start a pattern of exchange I simply couldn't, and wouldn't, keep up with. Would it be a Bratz doll? Polly Pocket? Barbie? Would I be tempted to start shopping at Wal-Mart to find just the right thing next year?

This is what the package contained: a shell; three tiny story books with the name Julia erased and the name Risa written over top; a deflated beach ball that Emily no longer needed; a beaded choker necklace; a pair of 3-D spectacles that created a nimbus of light around the objects you looked at through them; a handmade booklet and several pieces of construction paper cut into pleasing shapes. Risa delighted in each of the gifts. So did we!

Our friends in Ontario will laugh when they hear we're 'doing' Christmas. After all those years of resistance! We'll just have to explain that we're not doing Christmas; we're doing a Maritime Christmas. It's like going back to the fifties. Family is important here. It's a slower pace. It's…different.

My Moncton Christmas

CHRISTINE LOVELACE

WHEN I WAS THREE, my family (father, mother, brother and I) moved to Moncton, New Brunswick. We only lived there for nine years but those were the best years of my life.

I loved the summer, walking along the cracked cement sidewalks lined by bushy grass and old trees, and going to Centennial Park to ride the ponies. Summer meant weekend trips to Shediac where dad kept his sailboat. I liked walking to school on crisp fall mornings, entering the pillar-lined doorways of Edith Cavell School, long since burned down. However, winter was the season for my all-time favourite event in Moncton—Christmas.

The excitement would start growing as soon as the month of December started. It was very likely, being New Brunswick, that there would have already been one major snowfall. We built snow forts in the front yard. Building snow forts in the front yard took on a certain risk because they were closer to the road. Big machines chewing up the snow with whirling blades would come along the road, attacking the snowbanks and flinging a fine powder in the air from the chute at the top. We would thrill with the knowledge that one of us, if not careful, could accidentally be sucked up into the machine and meet our gory end.

Snowmen popped up everywhere. The heavy, moist snow was perfect for rolling out the large bottom, bulging middle and perfectly rounded head. Two rocks gathered from the driveway made large, dark eyes, and were used to form a slightly smiling mouth. Then a carrot was retrieved from the fridge crisper and used for a nose, followed by twig arms and an old scarf and toque to keep the snowman warm.

I cannot remember the specifics of the Santa Claus parade, but there were probably people sitting on flat wagons pulled by tractors or people waving from their large, 1970s cars. Maybe a high school band marched by, striking up a clanky rendition of "Rudolph the Red-nosed Reindeer." I do not really remember Santa, but I remember the feeling of waiting for him to appear and desperately having to pee but not wanting to go in my pink snowsuit. I would sing to myself in my head, to the tune of "We Wish you a Merry Christmas," "I don't need to go to the bathroom, I don't need to go the bathroom." It did not always work.

During the Christmas season, my parents would spend at least one or two evenings attending school pageants, enjoying the out of tune singing and bad re-creations of the nativity scene. It would be mitigated by their adult pursuits, as they would always have a Christmas party at their house with work colleagues and friends. I would get to join in for the first hour, proudly wearing my red-velvet dress and eating chips in glass bowls, the dip hanging in a smaller bowl perched precariously on the side.

Luckily, the adult Christmas party was not on the same night as the Charlie Brown Christmas special. Every time Linus told the story of the true meaning of Christmas for Charlie Brown, I would get a lump in my throat. That same night, my brother and I would write our letters to Santa Claus, making reasonable requests for bikes and "Easy-Bake Ovens," and then we would put a match to them and send our messages in a puff of smoke up the chimney and to the North Pole.

Finally, Christmas Eve would arrive. Christmas Day was, of course, a fulfillment of all the waiting. The presents would be unwrapped and the turkey dinner consumed. Then there would be visits to neighbours, and a trip to see the grandparents on their farm in Sackville. Maybe we would go ski-dooing or hitch the pony up to the sleigh, but to me, these activities were an anti-climax. Christmas Eve was the magical, glowing, shimmering high point of the entire year.

Mom would turn the lights off in the living room. A fire was started in the fireplace and candles lit. The only other light in the room would come from the Christmas tree, which we had chopped down ourselves from grandfather's woodlot.

The large bulbs would glow warmly, all red, blue and yellow, and the tree glittered with festoons of icicles. The air was scented with balsam or fir. Christmas music would be playing, perhaps Julie Andrews cooing about baby Jesus or Johnny Mathis telling us "friends were calling 'yoo-hoo.'"

Mom would let me get out the freezer-box cookies and put them in the oven. There would be ginger, orange, and cherry cookies. The cherry cookies had both red and green cherries, so that if you held them up to the light they appeared to be delicious stained glass. It is a wonder we did not go into a diabetic coma on Christmas Eve, because there would also be ribbon candy, candy canes and red barley candy shaped like roosters, which we sucked distractedly as we eyed the gifts under the tree. Dad's favourites were chicken bones from the Ganong factory, pink candy with chocolate inside.

My brother and I were allowed to open one present on Christmas Eve, probably as a valve to let off the steam of excitement building in our little heads. I always hoped I would open a book, although, strange child that I was, I would not have minded if it had been a new flannel nightdress. However, Mom would steer me to the right package, and I would spend the next hour or two reading my new Nancy Drew mystery. Finally, I would go to bed and marvel at the miracle that, on this night, a man would climb down our chimney and shower me with gifts.

Christmastime in the City

DAVID G. JONES

WHEN I BECAME A UNIVERSITY STUDENT, I discovered not only that there were many events and celebrations other than the ones that I had been instructed in, but also that there were different ways of celebrating the ones that I had known all my life.

I grew up in a Nova Scotia town where Christmas—perhaps *the* most important holiday of the year—was celebrated in two stages. First there was an extended family dinner where there was a *choice* of soft drinks and candies. Never mind the turkey with all the trimmings which was, after all, only food. The thrill was in having unbridled access to sugar. The best of all these sweet provocateurs was my Aunt Ada, who as near as I can determine, had a personal mission to make us all ruddy-cheeked, top and bottom.

In time, I would leave these small town experiences behind me. I left Cape Breton for Halifax to attend the University of King's College. I became an undergraduate at an institution that had been established almost 200 years before. What I discovered was the classic (and classical) ivy-covered college, students in academic gowns, a formal meal every evening, and more customs and traditions than I believed possible.

It was a shock to dress in jacket, tie and gown for dinners that began with Latin grace, experiencing a full place setting and a three-course meal. At home, one had soup or meat and potatoes, never both. I learned the practice of the old admonition: "No talk of sex, politics or religion during dinner please." We avoided contentious issues and stuck to what they call "light topics." We learned the gentle art of polite conversation.

Before I knew it, December arrived. I found myself immersed in term exams that I, like many others, was totally unprepared for. To get through this trial, we all had to study long into the night—every night. We went without everything but our books. We took on haggard looks, and experienced all sorts of sleep and food-deprived ailments. We were the walking dead.

When it seemed that we just might not survive this terrible ordeal, we were advised there would be a "King's at Home" in the Haliburton Room. What on earth was this? I wondered. I was told the university, in its *in loco parentis* role (in place of home and parents) would hold a Christmas celebration so that we might experience the friends and fellowship now being denied us. We had to work, though all of us were thinking of being home with our folks.

I was utterly unprepared for that evening. It began with one student reciting A. A. Milne's *King John's Christmas*—a child's poem. That was followed by another student reciting *A Child's Christmas in Wales*. Then another read one of Charles G. D. Roberts's animal stories. The event became quite hilarious when we all sang, with gusto, children's Christmas songs like "Frosty the Snowman" and "Rudolph the Red-nosed Reindeer." I was getting over my shock at seeing sophisticated university people sharing what were clearly child-like activities.

Then, things became much more subdued. Several students told interesting and somewhat humorous stories about their past Christmas experiences, all of which seemed very different than mine. Someone appeared at the piano. We sang carols—which now seem to me to have been not a little sad. Tears well when I think of how "Silent Night" and "Silver Bells" sounded that evening, as a fire crackled in the fireplace.

Cookies and hot cider were served, and I found us all clutching our mugs and reaching out to each other. I thought, as others must have, that we might just survive this

awful experience called "education." Too soon, it came to an
end. We broke off and drifted to our rooms to study once
again. Somehow though, our university—acting as our absent parents—had given us the courage to go on until we
could be re-united with our families…and once again have
our choice of soft drinks and candy.

What have I done?

DAVID DIVINE

WHEN I FLEW INTO HALIFAX from London, U.K. for the first
time, I didn't realize how important this city would become
in my future. I was due to speak at a national conference
on Black men and fatherhood. The terrain the plane passed
over in the last twenty minutes before touchdown brought
so many memories of my childhood in Aberlour orphanage, Scotland. I grew up there having been abandoned as
a child. I recall with happiness the people I came to see as
family and the buildings that became my home for some
eleven years.

From memory, the orphanage was surrounded by trees
and countryside and was located a short walk away from
water. During winter, occasionally when snow fell, it took
on for me, magical, warm, reflective tones. Add the lack of
human presence and those ingredients quietly, effortlessly,
emotionally open up images of childhood pleasures and
pain, friendship, loss, solitariness, and—funnily enough—
contentment, a childhood of sorts. Here I am now, ten
years after my speaking engagement, working and living
in Halifax, part of the way through the arduous process of
becoming a Canadian citizen. When I moved here in 2004,
everything was new: the English language spoken here, the
currency, how to collect mail, how to work the household

gadgets, where to catch a bus, trying to settle in and recreate the post to which I had been hired and the list goes on. It was exciting, too, especially experiencing "White Juan" which arrived a few weeks after my arrival, with its snow of fifty to seventy centimetres or more. Indeed, the city of Halifax virtually shut down for a week.

Looking out of my window into the front street, I saw the world of my childhood: silence, the lack of human presence, the beautiful landscapes of snow—pristine, not yet walked upon or ploughed, perched on branches lightly coating the upper parts. The snow balanced so precisely that the slightest breath would have dislodged the weight.

I was not prepared for the snow, the coldness of the winter which seemed to go on and on. I thought about how I could tell my wife and children back in the U.K.—in varying states of readiness and willingness to join me in eight months' time—about the shut down of the city. How could I tell them about the clear, beautiful whiteness that turns to a dirty grey, and which, no matter how positive one was, slowly seeps into one's skin and lodges there, passing into muscles, tendons, and bones, dragging you down? On the phone to the family I made light work of the weather, emphasizing the excitement, the shovelling of the snow at the front of the house which took me hours, and the loss of a layer of skin on my thumb. Everything appeared to be such an effort. It was like pushing a boulder up the hill all the time. I began to wonder how I could look into the eyes of my wife and children without asking myself, 'what have I done?' Has this been a walk too far? A task beyond my measure to tackle successfully? Condemned in a sense like a lot of other immigrants to hang on in there? The family arrived in the autumn, cautious, not quite trusting my all-too positive gloss on the Maritimes. New schools for the children, no work prospects for an overqualified partner, a difficult first year at university for my eldest, reconsideration of expectations honed endlessly prior to departure based on a diet of filtered reports from the front, and the tidying up of unfinished domestic business from a hesitant, but slowly emerging, final family decision to settle in Canada.

Christmas came and something special happened. Christmas celebration was confined to myself, my wife, and our three children. I cannot ever recall a Christmas where we did not have a significant number of other family members and friends around at some point over the holiday; however, it allowed us to have special time on our own to reflect upon Christmases past and the journeys we had all made to get to that point. It allowed the children to talk unencumbered about friends they missed, family members who were not present, and anxieties they had about coming to a new land where they knew nobody, in their late teens. It gave me the opportunity, as a very busy professional man who works long hours, to spend precious time in the company of my immediate family, freed from work demands, listening to how each family member felt about life.

During these conversations, the Christmas tree sparkled in the background. I can see us all now, in the living room. The tree was carried by my youngest son and I from the gardening centre at Canadian Tire, a quarter of a mile from our house. Christmas Day is normally spent quietly in our house, opening presents, preparing a late breakfast, enjoying one another's company, and watching some films. Telephone conversations took place with those family members and close friends who were thousands of miles away, and yes, there were some regrets about not being with them.

Christmas has always been very special to me from my days at the orphanage. Christmas then, as it is now, is a highlight of our year: a time for celebration and reflection, joy and forward-planning, a time for rest and recovery. In that sense, my first Christmas in the Maritimes changed little from previous Christmases. I saw the faint glow of obstacles overcome and found a new confidence and energy to tackle those as yet unseen. I accept that the gloss has slightly dulled on my initial expectations, but is replaced by a more enduring finish which will linger and fortify me. I believe we will stay in the Maritimes.

Dickens's A Christmas Carol is No Humbug

HARRY CHAPMAN

WHEN THE CHRISTMAS SEASON ROLLS AROUND, the Maritime airwaves and publications are filled with seasonal stories for young and old alike. My personal all-time favourite is Charles Dickens's *A Christmas Carol*, a book I never tire of reading and whose message is as relevant today as it was when it first appeared more than 160 years ago.

First published in London on December 19, 1843, it was a runaway best-seller. By Christmas, 6,000 copies had been sold and by January 9,000 copies were in print.

The principal character, Ebenezer Scrooge, one of the most vilified figures in English literature, is described in the early paragraphs as "a squeezing, wrenching, grasping, scraping, clutching, covetous old sinner."

A rather harsh indictment, since Scrooge eventually changes his life from the "covetous old sinner" to everyone's good friend and neighbour. As the author says, "he became as good a friend, as good a master, as good a man, as the good old city knew or any other good old city, town, or borough in the good old world."

It's Scrooge's conversion or "reclamation" from sinner to saint that makes *A Christmas Carol* a most appealing and endearing tale. This transformation occurs during a Christmas Eve of ghostly visitations.

When Dickens wrote *A Christmas Carol* he was thirty-one years old and in need of money. His previous novel, *Martin Chuzzlewit,* was not a best-seller and in order to recoup some of his diminished income, Dickens wrote *A Christmas Carol* in six weeks.

Dickens provides his readers with an insight into Scrooge's flawed character at the very outset. His nephew's invitation to Christmas dinner is rudely rejected and his nephew's wish for a Merry Christmas is returned with a scowling "bah humbug."

When two men visit his office to solicit a contribution "to buy some meat, drink, and means of warmth for the poor," Scrooge informs them "he can't afford to make idle people merry," then shows them the door.

Bob Cratchit requests to have Christmas Day off, pointing out that Christmas only comes once a year. Scrooge counters with "it's a poor excuse for picking a man's pockets every December 25."

Dickens has set the table for the literary feast that is to follow. It is while he is alone at home that Scrooge's journey of reclamation begins. His first ghostly visitor is Jacob Marley, his former business partner, and a man as equally mean-spirited when he was alive. Marley appears shackled in chains and cash boxes suffering a tormented eternity as

a result of his past life and his devotion to money. His visit is not a social call; it's more of a wake up call, a warning of a similar fate unless Scrooge changes his way of life. Before Marley's spirit departs, he tells Scrooge he will be haunted during the night by three other spirits.

The first, the Ghost of Christmas Past, takes Scrooge on a journey back to his earlier life at boarding school, his apprenticeship with Mr. Fezziwig, and the ending of his relationship with his fiancée Belle.

The second visitor, the Ghost of Christmas Present, leads Scrooge through the streets of London on Christmas morning where cheerful people greet each other with the joy and happiness of the season. The stroll ends at Bob Cratchit's home where he and his family are about to eat their Christmas dinner. It is here Scrooge sees Tiny Tim, Cratchit's disabled youngest son who, according to the spirit, will not see many more Christmases if his present situation remains unchanged.

With the Ghost of the Future, Scrooge witnesses the Cratchit family's grief following the death of Tiny Tim and his own death which no one mourns. Scrooge is led to a lonely cemetery where a headstone sits engraved with his own name.

At this point Scrooge realizes that his pursuit of personal wealth at the expense of others has been a wasted life, a lonely life without love or friends and he begs the ghost for a second chance, an opportunity to mend his ways and start his life anew.

Scrooge awakens from his tormented sleep on Christmas Day to find that he is alive and back in his own bedchamber. He leaps from his bed a new man, a changed man, now resolved to do good in the world.

He sends a large turkey to the Cratchit family, and he meets the men whom he brusquely turfed out of this office the previous day and offers them a sizeable donation to help the poor and destitute. He visits his nephew and accepts the invitation to dinner. He raises Bob Cratchit's salary and provides help for Tiny Tim so he does not die as earlier forecast by the ghost.

Like most of Dickens's stories, *A Christmas Carol* has a happy ending. It was the first of many Christmas stories by Dickens but it is by far the most popular.

Since the story first appeared in print, it has been told and retold in many forms. It has been dramatized on stages around the world and presented in children's picture books and animated cartoons. Several movie versions have been filmed, and numerous variations on the Scrooge theme appear each season on television. My favourite movie version is the 1951 British film with Alastir Sim as Scrooge. The often-reprinted story eventually brought Dickens huge financial rewards and his dramatic readings earning him more money than any of his other books.

Ebenezer Scrooge was created many years ago but his story is very much alive today and will continue to live for many years into the future. He is a reminder to all that Christmas is a time of goodwill and sharing with others that should be celebrated all year long.

Christmas should be, as Tiny Tim remarked, a blessing for everyone, not a "humbug."

Waking Angie

HARVEY SAWLER (based on an idea from Ann Kenney)

ANGIE WAS THE EARLY RISER in the Duffy clan. Three hundred and sixty-four days of the year, she was up and at it; each and every day that is, except Christmas morning.

Andrew, twins Bryan and Glen, Ned, Candy and Pauline—the other Duffy kids in oldest-to-youngest chronological order—had a way of accelerating Christmas morning by rushing to the brightly-decorated mantel, where their stockings hung, and then to the gifts under the tree. Their objective was to open everything with utmost dispatch, as though ridding themselves of the burden of wonder they'd carried since the mid-August appearance of the Sears *Wish Book*.

Since the age of four, Angie had refused to get out of bed on Christmas morning. She very simply, matter-of-factly, refused to get up. And to the frustration of her brothers and sisters, her parents—Barney and Flora—refused to do anything about it. It was a matter to be decided amongst siblings, they said.

Angie wasn't suffering from vertigo or a chemical im-balance. After looking forward to Christmas for so many months, weeks, days and hours, Angie had learned first-hand that the big moment could evaporate in the little time it takes to make toast. No sooner would it start than it would end—that special-ness; that magical moment of Christmas zapped out of sight and lodged into memory. She came to realize this when she was three, precipitating a flood of tears after the gifts were opened.

"What's wrong little angel?" asked Barney.

"I want it to last all the time," she blubbered, drawing a gallon of sympathy from both mom and dad and laughter from her brothers and sisters.

"Everyone's in a big hurry."

Once the initial rush of Christmas subsided, all that re-mained were dreamy visions of the next one to come, an enormous three hundred and sixty-five sleeps away.

The year she turned four, Angie decided that from then on, she would postpone getting up for as long as possible on Christmas morning. She would lie in bed with her quilt pulled tightly up to her chin and over and over in her mind she would explore her red and green stocking trimmed with white marabou and the little surprises therein. She was de-termined to make these Christmas things last. Putting it off seemed the only logical way of going about it.

There was a problem, of course, with Angie's refusals. They lacked consensus. The Duffys had an unwritten house rule that was strictly enforced. No one went into the living room, near the stockings or near the gifts until everyone was ready to go in together. So in that first year of Angie's refusal, the impatient collective of Andrew, Bryan and Glen, Ned, Candy and Pauline crammed into the doorway of her room.

"Hurry up Angie!" said Candy. "The hardwood floor is cold out here."

"I can't get up or it'll be all over," said Angie defiantly, eyes clenched as she tried to block out the intrusion of her brothers and sisters into her private Christmas-ness.

"It'll be over all right if you don't get up," said twins Bryan and Glen in stereo. They were widely acknowledged as the pair most capable of conjuring up a plan regardless of the circumstance.

When Angie rebuffed them a second and then a third time, the twins conspired and huddled the others together in the hall. Not a moment later, four boys and two girls were pouncing on her bed, tearing away her quilt, joined by an overly excited, bouncing, wildly barking Axel, the family's fluffy collie dog. As Candy and Pauline held their sister to the mattress, the boys struggled to place the chilly bottoms of their feet up against their sister's legs and back. It was hard for Barney and Flora to stay in bed hearing their "helpless little yelper" cry out for help, but they knew that this too was a matter amongst siblings. The twins' plan worked and the entire Duffy brood was soon in the hall outside Barney and Flora's bedroom door. Angie stood with the group, but with her arms defiantly folded and her eyes clenched, dreading the thought that the biggest moment of the year was about to self-destruct like a *Mission Impossible* tape.

And so was born an odd family tradition. When she was five, six, seven, eight and nine, Angie refused to get up on

Christmas morning. And even as they in turn got older, Andrew, Bryan and Glen, Ned, Candy and Pauline conspired in the hallway for new and more devilish ways to force their sister from her bed. But none of the ploys worked. Only the dreaded sensation of cold feed on Angie's back and legs was certain to force her from the bed.

Then, the Christmas after Angie turned ten, something unusual happened. Barney and Flora listened for the throng to gather outside Angie's room, anticipating the bustle, clamour and laughter of the older children using their chilly feet to raise Angie from her bed. But after the shuffling, mumbling sound of the gathering, there was a strange sense of quiet, followed by the appearance of six faces, peering around the doorframe of Barney and Flora's bedroom.

"Angie's not in bed," said Andrew.

"We think she's been kidnapped," said Bryan and Glen naughtily and in stereo.

Barney looked at Flora and came to a realization. Their "helpless little yelper," wasn't so little any more.

"No, not kidnapped," Barney corrected Bryan and Glen, chuckling. "I'd say Angie has decided to start a new Christmas tradition. I think it's called 'getting the better of my brothers and sisters.'"

Andrew turned and drew Bryan, Glen, Ned, Candy and Pauline into another brief assembly in the hallway. For fifteen minutes, they scoured the Duffy household, unable to find any sign of Angie.

They were ready to give up the search when Pauline noticed that Axel was missing too. Just as he had one other time after a memorable visit to the vet, it was Axel who blew the cover. There, scrunched up inside the floor-level cupboard, where she hadn't hidden in seven years, was Angie with the turncoat dog.

From their bedroom, Barney and Flora heard a burst of children's yelling and laughter, followed by the charge of sixteen feet and four paws bombarding the stairs. Led by Bryan and Glen, the six older Duffy kids chased Angie back to her bed, where they proceeded to torture her, as was tradition, with their very cold feet. When Angie finally gave in, the group of eight, which included Axel, gathered outside Barney and Flora's bedroom door.

"Is it time yet, Angie?" Barney asked.

Against her will, with her arms folded and her eyes clenched in predictable anticipation, Angie nodded and conceded to her father. Moments later, with the stockings emptied and the gifts opened and spread across the living room floor, Angie began thinking about the next Christmas to come, three hundred and sixty-five frustrating sleeps away. And about a better place for her and Axel to hide.

The Christmas Tree and Decorations

"It happens every autumn as if on cue. As soon as the nights begin to lengthen and the air begins to nip, homeowners begin to untangle strings of outside lights and mount them on the eaves of their homes. Soon whole communities join in this activity, decorating public trees, buildings and streets with tiny lights and greenery adorned with bright red bows. Once the outside is decorated to the homeowner's satisfaction, the transformation begins inside. The furniture in the living room or family room is rearranged to make room for the Christmas tree. Boxes of treasured ornaments appear from the basement, saved from year to year and used to turn the tree into a piece of family art. Wreathes and boughs, candles and bowls of shiny baubles are added to mantels in an attempt to drive away the winter darkness and fill the home with light.

Before the days of artificial trees, families made finding the perfect tree an adventure. Many remember taking the car to a farm, or bundling up the children and hauling the young ones on a sled as they tramped through the woods to look for the perfect tree. Mothers wanted one that had all the sides just the same and a perfect tapered point at the top.

Each family has its own idea of how the tree should be decorated. Some families buy or make a new ornament to add to the tree every year. In years gone by, the tree was often in the porch when the children went to bed. When they woke up on Christmas morning it was trimmed—by the Christmas angel.

Years ago my mother whipped up a light paste of Ivory soap powder and sprinkled it on the branches to make them look like they still had snow on them. Every decoration had to be placed on in proper order. First she looped the shiny tin-selled rope to hide any imperfections in the tree's shape, followed by the delicate glass balls and birds. She placed a silver star at the top of the tree and lit candles on Christmas Eve to provide the light. However, the tree wasn't finished yet. Long after my brothers and I were tucked in bed, Mother added silver icicles to every limb of the tree. Each icicle was hung individually then straightened so it would catch the light of the candles. The icicles added a shimmering glow like the light of the sun dancing off tree branches in the forest after an ice storm.

Christmas Rites

BETH POWNING

Just before sunset we ski up to get the tree. We've already chosen it, to avoid the dreadful family arguments we used to have a few years ago.

In the blue shadows it stands as still and snow-laden as all the others. Already, Jake and I feel remorse. Neither of us wants to do the actual cutting, so Peter takes off his skis and kneels in the snow. I knock snow off the branches with my ski pole and push against the trunk as he saws, feeling the strange moment when the tree is no longer elastic and tensile but falls forward into the air.

Going back down the hill, we ski into the sunset, snow flying up around us. Jake hauls the tree on the toboggan. The moon rises. Grown from its shell-like fragility to a commanding fullness, it pulses up behind the spruce trees and slides blue-silver into the sky.

When we arrive at the house, there are stars over the barn and the cats are waiting for us, twitchy-tailed. We drag the tree into the house. Its presence transforms the hall, the kitchen, and the dining room as it passes through. It sheds bark, resin, needles, and a forest essence comprising the tree's long communion with wind, earth, and sun. In the cold, icy fragrance is a sense of darkness and silence. We'll sweep up later. Clutter is part of the process. The couch is swivelled out of place, branch tips laid on its cushions. The floor is strewn with lopsided shoeboxes: out of them we lift glass balls, strands of red and silver beads, starched embroidered stars. The room smells of the popcorn-cranberry chains I loop from branch to branch. Peter stands on a chair and hangs his favourite ornament, a plastic banana, from the tree's tip. Jake and I object, as always, but he insists it's a crescent moon. "Okay, that's enough decoration," says

Jake, finally. We go around the house, turning off lights so we can see how the tree reflects in the glass doors of the sunroom, how its lights gleam on the cranberries and fold in the earlobe curves of the popcorn.

It lives in me all year—the memory of this moment when the tree becomes a symbol with a power out of all proportion to its elements. I lie on the couch, arms crossed behind my head. The room smells of balsam, the taste of Christmas when I nibble a fir needle in summer. I think of the ancient peoples who performed such rituals of transformation, making one thing imitate another to gain control over what they feared.

Jake and I put on our coats and go out onto the lawn. We stand under the maples and look back at the house. Without its lights, the house loses its inner energy. It's simply a square box. In the moonlight I can imagine it abandoned and empty. Only one window is lighted by the Christmas tree, which sparkles cold as starlight, but I can also see the firelike warmth of its glistening red balls. It shines across the fields, deeply familiar, profoundly human, framed by the window—as if you could put hope in a box, hold it steady, make it visible.

Nova Scotia Christmas Tree Hunt

CHRISTINA FLEMMING

Each year at Christmastime, supermarket parking lots glitter with strings of multicoloured lights and ring with the chatter of excited families inspecting Christmas trees. The smell of pine, and sometimes apple cider, fills the cold air. Many families have their own distinct tradition when it comes to choosing the perfect tree. Growing up in Nova Scotia, I have experienced the old-fashioned art of Christmas tree hunting.

It felt just like a theme park ride, bumping along on the back of my great uncle's truck. This was adventure. Eight years old, I was the king of the road (or rather, queen of the road). It was just my father and me clutching the sides of the huge Ford truck as we bounced over the rugged road through the woods. The cold winter wind whipped against our faces. The crisp December weather didn't bother me; the prospect of choosing the perfect Christmas tree was too exciting. My mother and great uncle Arnie were warm inside the cab of the truck.

My uncle could have navigated the dirt road in his sleep. Unlike the rest of us, he was thinking about Christmas trees all year long. Even in the summer. In fact, all year round he worked outdoors pruning the trees to ensure the perfect shape. Uncle Arnie owned the acres of land we were flying over in the truck. He was the Christmas tree man in our family.

"Hold on tight," my dad shouted above the noise. He was protective of his only daughter but wouldn't deny me the experience of riding in the back of the truck. I squinted into the sunlight as the truck emerged from a shadowy portion of road and continued traveling through expansive hills dotted with perfectly groomed trees. The ground was concealed by muddy clumps of snow and marked by the footsteps of men removing trees. Arnie's trees were shipped all over the United States, some even ended up in Florida.

When we pulled to a stop Arnie and my mother hopped out of the cab. My father had to jump down and lift me from the back of the truck. "Look over there," Arnie said in a hushed tone. His rough workman's hand pointed through a clump of trees. Gliding through the woods, we saw a deer. Having been devastated by the movie *Bambi*, I immediately fell in love with the beautiful creature, so light on its feet, pale brown in colour. The deer was oblivious to our venture to recreate a tiny piece of its natural surroundings in our living room. Arnie was long desensitized by the animals, having seen them many times, but for us seeing a deer was a sacred experience.

Arnie led us through the woods carrying a saw. I wondered why we couldn't just pick the tree like a flower. He led us toward a tall tree marked with a yellow plastic ribbon. The ribbon was to warn other tree cutters that this tree was off limits, selected especially for us.

"I like it!" I said triumphantly.

"It's a big tree," my father agreed with admiration.

"I don't know." My mother was never satisfied with the first tree she saw.

"Well there's another one I marked, just in case you didn't want this fella," Arnie said patiently. Imagining I was an ice princess gliding through her winter forest, I skipped through the trees. The next tree was twelve feet tall. Our ceiling is eleven feet high.

"It's perfect!" my mother gasped.

"It might be a bit too big," Arnie warned.

"I like it!" I said.

"Well I suppose we could cut the bottom off her and see if she'd fit," my dad said.

"I knew you like big trees but I wasn't sure if this would be too big or not."

"No. It's not!" my mom said enthusiastically. After a

few minutes of debating, the men started to saw the tree down. Standing beside my mother, I watched with widened eyes as the tree fell.

The monstrous tree took up the entire back of the Ford. On the way home, we all crammed in the cab of the truck. My little heart was bursting with excitement. I wasn't thinking about Christmas morning and the brightly wrapped presents under the tree, instead I was filled with love and pride for being related to the Christmas tree man. I couldn't wait to tell my friends from school about the deer and show them the big tree in our living room. Smiling from ear to ear, I glanced back to peek at the tree. It was gone. I thought maybe it was my imagination playing tricks on me.

"Um, Dad?"

"Yes dear."

"The tree is gone."

"Don't joke about things like that," he said, glancing back.

"It must have fallen off the back of the truck!" my father shouted after realizing I wasn't joking. Arnie laughed a hearty laugh.

"Oh no!" my mother wailed. I wasn't sure whether to laugh or burst into tears. Arnie swung the truck around and we headed back to claim the tree in the road.

When we collected the tree from the middle of the road, our travails were far from over. It took all three of us to hold the tree steady while my father attempted to screw it into the industrial stand. My mother worried that a miniature forest of animals would jump from the depths of the green branches spreading across the living room. To decorate the twelve foot tree, we had to use a step ladder. Visitors always gasped at the sheer size. The ceiling was forever marked with a faint green streak from where the top of the tree scraped as we attempted to shove our snowman on top. But even after a few setbacks, we wouldn't have wanted any other tree in the world.

The Perfect Tree

ALAN SYLIBOY

CHRISTMAS IN THE 1950S AND 60S was a major undertaking on the Mi'kmaq reserve of Millbrook where I grew up. Our community was small then, with only about thirty houses, so I knew every person who lived there. Most people were kind, some were bad-tempered, and some held grudges against each other the rest of the year but put them aside at Christmas.

Midnight mass on Christmas Eve was the big event of the year. The mystical celebration began with the tolling of the bell signalling everyone to make their way to the church. There was ceremony and incense, mass was chanted in Latin, and the choir sang songs in Mi'kmaq. This was all very powerful to a young native boy.

My mother, Teresa, considered Christmas to be a year-round activity. She played Christmas music of the era on the stereo in our house at any time—albums by the Mormon Tabernacle Choir, Perry Como, Mario Lanza, and Frank Sinatra. My mother was very careful with the little money she earned as a housekeeper in the nearby town of Truro and put gifts on layaway in the stores. It took her all year to pay for them but she made sure we all had something we wanted. My younger brother Dale and I might not have had a lot of presents or our stockings completely filled, but we felt like millionaires for a few days. There were always some new toys and clothes. We seldom got grapes, oranges, or bananas during the rest of the year but they were in abundance at Christmas. No one told us kids to stop or take it easy. We were allowed to eat whatever we wanted and to do whatever we wanted; discipline was suspended for Christmas. My mother planned all year so that we would have presents, good food, and a family tradition to follow.

She was very inspired by Christmas and expected the rest of us to rise to the occasion.

For the men in the family that meant hunting for the perfect tree, starting long before Christmas arrived. This was before cultivated trees were sold in nearly every parking lot so there was no easy way out of this Christmas tree business for us. My stepfather Lawrence took me on his hunting trips and we were always looking out for a good tree as well as game. If we saw a promising tree we would mark the spot or remember it and come back closer to Christmas. Lawrence did his best to teach me how to hunt rabbits but I was a bit of a failure. I got one kill under my belt, so to speak, but that set me off hunting forever. I really could not kill a rabbit or anything else after that. I am sure I was a disappointment to Lawrence but he did not seem to hold that against me. Fortunately I was better at hunting trees.

We sometimes found a good candidate but it might be fifty feet high. We were really only after the top six feet, not the whole tree. The tops of the taller trees get uniform sunlight on all sides, so they are more symmetrical and fuller than shorter trees growing in more shaded conditions. We would chop one of these massive trees down only to find that the top had too many flaws that had not been apparent from the ground looking up, a big hole on one side or too many bad branches. The perfect tree had branches coming out at right angles, evenly spaced with no deformities. The taller the tree, the thicker the trunk, making it much heavier than a young six-foot tree. If we found a good one we took turns dragging it out of the woods—sometimes for a couple of miles. It was often loaded with cones that only added to its weight. We had to go across brooks and streams, over frozen fields, and across a highway to get it home. The tree often got banged up and damaged in the process unless there was a good snow cover to slide it on.

Finally, the moment arrived when my mother would come out of the house and have a look at the tree. She had great expectations and the standard was always quite high. Sometimes she was not at all impressed. She would not say it out loud but her body language told us plenty. If we did not get the reaction we were hoping for, I would try to make a case for the tree. If we turned it around this way or that way maybe we could make it work, I would say, but this did not usually sway her at all. She had the perfect tree in mind and this was not it! We had to go back and try to find a better one.

Eventually a tree would pass my mother's inspection and make it into the house. She took over from there, decorating it with the old family ornaments from past Christmases and a few new ones, putting the beautifully wrapped presents underneath, setting the scene for the season. Christmas then became rounds of visiting with family and friends, sharing food, stories, and good times. The perfect tree became a symbol for the continuity of Christmases past and future, and a sense of belonging to family and community.

The Wreath-Making Tradition

LAURA BEST

IT'S TREEING TIME. If you say that where I come from everyone knows exactly what you mean and not only does it take in the harvesting of Christmas trees but wreath making as well. Traditionally, treeing time was the latter part of October although today some companies put off treeing until the first of November to ensure less shedding and a fresher product.

In East Dalhousie, there is scarcely a household where Christmas wreaths were not made at one time or another. Bordering on Lunenburg County, which just so happens to have been officially named the Christmas tree capital of the world back in 1996, it is no wonder this industry spilled over into our area.

It was not until the 1960s that the making of Christmas wreaths became popular in our area. I'm told that before that time individuals sometimes hung wreaths on their door during the Christmas season although from what one lady told me it was obviously not all that common. She said that a visitor once saw the wreath she had hanging on the front door and asked if someone had passed away.

Christmas trees and wreaths stacked in people's yards was a common sight during treeing season when I was growing up and this is still true even today. Women were recruited to make wreaths to be shipped to the U.S. market. While men headed into their private woodlots with axes in hand to cut Christmas trees, women went along to gather brush for wreath making. Often times the brush was clipped off the trees in the woods and brought home in burlap bags.

Once supper was over and the dishes were washed, it was time to get to work. Rings, wire and clippers were a wreath-maker's tools, along with a flat surface to work on. Whereas women were traditionally the wreath makers of the family, many hand-tied wreaths were wound right on the kitchen table in times past, and women tell stories of working well into the wee hours of the morning to complete an order.

And what did these women receive for all their efforts at that time? The tidy sum of twenty-five cents a piece was paid for a twelve-inch wreath and was considered by many women to be good money. A neighbour of mine recalls the first year she made wreaths and says quite proudly, "That first year I made seventy-five dollars and I bought a mattress for on my bed." Other women tell similar stories of using their money either for Christmas presents or to purchase some new item for the home.

I can remember coming home from school and seeing my own parents winding wreaths in our kitchen. Little did

I know back then that I, too, would be a wreath maker in years to come. Today, wreaths produced on machines are replacing those tied by hand, and as an older generation of wreath makers retires there are few "younger people" taking up the craft. Naturally, more wreaths can be produced on a machine, although I much prefer the look of a handmade wreath. Somehow treeing season doesn't seem quite the same if I don't make at least a few dozen wreaths by hand.

The art of hand-tying wreaths is a tradition that is slowly coming to an end but I'm sure that as long as there is Christmas in Lunenburg County there will be somebody, somewhere, hand-winding brush around a ring.

A Christmas Wreath in the Black Tradition

JOLEEN GORDON

SOME YEARS AGO, I took an evening class with my basketry teacher and mentor, Mrs. Edith Clayton, learning how to make the Christmas wreaths well known in the communities of Cherry Brook and East Preston. It was a wonderful introduction, not only to the folklore of her people, but also to the seasonal variety of colourful wild plants we have growing here in Nova Scotia.

Mrs. Clayton began collecting the plants needed for wreath making in mid-summer when the pearly everlasting flowers, *Anaphalis margaritacea*, were in bloom along the roadsides and in open spaces. These delicate white flowers were picked while the flower heads were still tightly curled into small white balls. She bound handfuls of flowers together with string and hung them upside down so the heads would dry upright. Some of the flowers were dyed by dipping them in a dye bath—purple was a favourite colour—and then re-dried upside down.

In the early fall, the rose hips were ready to harvest. There are many types and sizes of wild rose hips in Nova Scotia, but the preferred ones for wreaths were the medium-sized hips on the wild rose bush, *Rosa rugosa*, found growing along roadsides and by the seacoast. Mrs. Clayton would cut small lengths of the stems and her children would carefully remove all the thorns with their small fingers. The hips were stored in paper bags until they were needed.

Shortly before wreath-making season began in late October, the men went into the woods to gather the fresh material needed for the wreaths. One straight and unbranched piece of the flexible woodland shrub witherod, *Viburnum cassinoides*, was cut for each wreath. For the greenery, the community used to gather the feathery green clubmoss known as evergreen or ground pine, *Lycopodium obscurum*, and branches of the fragrant evergreen balsam fir tree, *Abies balsamea*. Another woodland plant which was freshly gathered for the wreaths was the soft and puffy creamy-white lichen commonly known as reindeer moss, *Cladonia*.

Wreath making was a communal affair. Men, women, and often their children gathered together in their homes to make the wreaths which were an important source of income. For some years in the 1980s, Mrs. Clayton taught wreath making to a group of city folks from the Halifax library in her home. Her workshop table was covered with two- to three-foot lengths of witherod sticks, a huge mound of two- to three-inch pieces of aromatic evergreen fir boughs, a basket of moist fluffy lichen, another filled with two- to three-inch stems of ruby red rosehips, bunches of two- to three-inch stems of dried pearly everlasting flowers, and a ball of cotton string.

To make the foundation of the wreath, we bent the witherod stick into a circle the desired size of the wreath. The inner surfaces of the two overlapping ends of the witherod were shaved so the ring was the same sized diameter all around; Mrs. Clayton thankfully did all the knife cutting with her strong, steady hands. The only tools we used were our fingers as we bound the overlapped ends tightly together with a piece of string.

To add the greenery, we first tied a two-foot length of string to the circle of witherod ring. Then we placed one small piece of greenery on top of the ring with two small pieces on either side and bound the greenery tightly to the ring three or four times. We bound another bunch of greenery about an inch further along the ring with the same length of string. We repeated adding and binding around the ring, tying on a new piece of string when needed.

To add the woodland lichen, flowers and rose hips to the ring, we placed a sprig of colour in the middle of two pieces of greenery before binding. Sometimes, we added the rosehips and lichen together so the red rosehips rested on the cloud of billowy white lichen. Some wreaths had only greenery and rosehips; others had flowers and lichen.

In this way, bunches of greenery and colour were added to the entire ring of witherod, pulling aside the first bunch to fit in the last bunch and completely covering the ring of witherod. The end of the string was looped around the wreath and knotted for hanging.

The wreaths were all so beautiful and all so varied; no two were alike. The colours of red and green and white were visually stimulating which, combined with the resin aroma of the fresh greenery, made a wonderful sensual experience. The moment called for a cup of tea and a lunch.

The wreaths continue to be sold by members of the Black community at the Halifax Farmers' Market and door-to-door in some areas of the city during the Christmas season. They are a beautiful natural Christmas decoration reminding us of the glorious variety of woodland plants we have growing here in Nova Scotia.

Will We Have A Christmas Tree This Year?

ROGER CYR

SNOW ARRIVED EARLY in Nova Scotia the year my Uncle Donald stayed with my grandmother and me at our Cumberland County farm. By early December the wind was roaring up the Bay of Fundy, bringing snow ahead of its wintry blast and rattling the windowpanes in our house. The line fence below the house had disappeared under a white blanket which grew thicker with each snowfall and the road to Parrsboro was blocked with waist high drifts. If this kept up we'd be marooned for two or three days at a time. My mother was away working in Truro and would not arrive home until Christmas Eve. Four days before Christmas of 1940 the wind began blowing from the south and the temperature in our valley rose above the freezing point for the first time in weeks. On the twenty-third freezing rain and sleet followed and covered the roads with a thick blanket of ice. With the roads covered with ice and snow I was afraid that the bus would not arrive and she would not spend the holidays with me. I had marked off each day on a calendar that hung under the clock on the wall in anticipation of her arrival and the gifts I was hoping she would bring.

At four o'clock in the afternoon after I had helped my Uncle Donald tend to our domestic animals and fill the woodbox behind the kitchen stove. (Donald supported us by cutting and selling firewood from a stand of trees that grew at the top of the hill that overlooked our house. Each morning he harnessed our horse to a sled and made his way to the woodlot. At four o'clock each day he returned with the sled filled to capacity and after supper he delivered the wood to customers in Parrsboro where he received five dollars.) I stood with my nose pressed against the window that faced the road. Very few cars were moving but my grandmother reassured me that the bus would arrive on time. By four-thirty the ugly dark clouds hanging over our rooftops began to break up and we could see a red sun sinking at the western end of our valley.

Just as darkness fell I saw headlights crest the hill a mile to the east and the bus crossed the bridge spanning the river that marked our boundary. "She's here," I screamed and sprang for the door, not taking the time to pull on my coat. I ran to the road just as the bus slid to a stop. She had a large carton of gifts which Donald carried to the house and we all sat around the kitchen table with everyone trying to talk at once.

But even though my mother was home, Christmas wasn't complete. Although Donald had walked to the neighbours and brought home a goose for my grandmother to prepare for Christmas dinner, he had neglected to cut a Christmas tree. After supper he lit the lantern and we walked to where two small spruce trees were fighting the north wind for survival. He selected the larger and with one swipe of a well-honed axe he severed the trunk. (For years afterwards I watched the other tree grow ever so slowly, as if it was missing its mate. One year when I was home on leave from the air force I saw that the tree was gone—I have always hoped it became a Christmas tree too.) Once home, we took the decorations from the closet and everyone helped trim the tree and arrange the gifts around the base. It was one of my best Christmases ever and I have never forgotten the year my mother braved a winter storm and slippery roads to spend the holidays with her family.

Deck the Tree with Memories

JOAN DAWSON

IT IS A FEW DAYS BEFORE CHRISTMAS; the sweet-scented fir tree that one of my grandsons has helped me choose has been brought in and stands in its traditional spot, and I have carried the boxes of ornaments up from the basement. For me, decorating the tree is a well-loved annual ritual. I start by getting out all the tapes and CDs of Christmas music that have been gathering dust since the previous December, and choose a suitable accompaniment before beginning the task. First, the strings of lights are installed, and then I dip into the decoration boxes. Mine is not a "designer" Christmas tree such as one sees in glossy magazines. It is a tree of memories, and as I hang each ornament it brings to mind a person, an event or a place connected to past Christmases in Nova Scotia.

Christmas baubles are by their nature fragile, but some of mine are well-travelled survivors which came from my late husband's family. They made the journey from his childhood Christmases in Saskatoon, via Toronto where he grew up, and Ottawa where his parents later lived, to arrive eventually in the old family home in Bridgewater. When our children were small, we used to go to Bridgewater to visit my mother-in-law each Christmastime. There, a splendid tree always graced the large entrance hall.

As I hang some of its surviving ornaments on my own tree, I remember that in those days, Christmases in Bridgewater were always white. After a fresh snowfall, the Dawson family home, with its barn and carriage house among the trees, formed a perfect Christmas card image.

I hang more decorations: glass balls, each with a name written on it. Some of these date back to 1960, my first Christmas in Nova Scotia. My professor husband had come "home" after five years in exile at the University of

Manitoba. He was teaching at King's, and we were offered accommodation in a house on Coburg Road, which we shared with ten female students for whose well-being we were responsible to the Dean of Women. Towards the end of term, we decided to put up a Christmas tree at the foot of the wide staircase, which made a perfect setting. In those days, King's was also an Anglican theological college and we were given to understand that "anticipating Christmas" was rather frowned upon while we were supposed to be observing Advent in a suitably low-key mood. But we reckoned that exams were penitential enough for our charges, and besides, if we waited until Christmas they would all have gone home. So up went the tree.

This was our first big tree, and the few baubles we had purchased in Winnipeg were far from sufficient to do it justice, so we bought boxes of coloured glass balls to add to the collection. I don't remember who had had the idea of writing on each ball the name of a member of our extended "family," including of course the dog, but as I hang the balls up year after year, I see the faces of those students, some of whom have become life-long friends.

After we moved into our own home, the custom of writing names on the Christmas tree balls continued. Our children, our dogs, our Christmas guests, human and canine, and more recently our grandchildren—everyone who has been with us at Christmastime is remembered. As I hang the balls, I think of my father, who loved to spend Christmas in Halifax with us after my mother died, and made the annual journey from England until he was well into his nineties. I think of a young Dalhousie student from South Africa who could not get home for the vacation and came to us for Christmas dinner. I think of Dinah, the border collie who spent the holiday with us one year when her owner had to be away, and still comes into my house as if she owns it. And I remember many others who have eaten their turkey and Christmas pudding at our table, absent friends and those who are no longer with us.

Some of the ornaments were painstakingly manufactured by children and grandchildren; some were gifts from friends, some were bought at school fairs and craft shows. There are glass hummingbirds and peace doves and a cardinal with real feathers. There are eggs decorated with bright fabrics and gold braid. There are wooden angels, and straw angels, and angels made of metallic foil. Among several ornaments fashioned in pewter, I find a tiny model of the Little Dutch Church, where many of the early citizens of Halifax celebrated Christ's birth. And here is the old town clock that has witnessed Halifax Christmases for over two hundred years. And finally, above them all, I set the star brought back from England after a sabbatical during which we spent Christmas in Oxford.

The tree is decorated and the boxes put away until twelfth night. The loose needles have been swept up and the Provençal nativity figures set out. There are still cookies and mince pies to make, but they can wait. It's time to put on a different CD, pour a glass of wine, and enjoy another beautiful Christmas tree.

The Magic of Tinsel

DARLENE LAWSON

IT HAPPENS EVERY YEAR. I stand in the craft section of a shop, looking at the rows of ribbon wondering which one I will choose to decorate my tree. I admire the burgundy, gold and blue ribbons I see on other trees and the different colours of beads now used for decorating are certainly dazzling. Over the years, I've brought home many different ribbons and envisioned how beautiful my new designer tree would be. Then I take out the box of decorations, telling myself "don't look in that bag." But always, lovingly packed on the very top, is my bag full of tinsel. And I know I can't resist. For every year as I hold the tinsel in my hands, just like magic, I'm transported back.

Back to our country home in Bass River, Kent County, and an early December 24th morning as Daddy brought home the Christmas tree. Back to the time when a polished oil lamp sat on the kitchen table providing light and tinsel was the decoration that lit up our tree. Back to the smell of brown bread baking in the wood cookstove mingling with the smell of freshly cut fir as my sisters and I tediously hung the tinsel one by one under Daddy's watchful eye. Back to the days when we visited from house to house to see who had the most perfect tinselled tree. Back to the night when the moon was full in the sky, the fields were covered with a crust of snow, and Daddy would tell Mom and me we were going to visit Everett and Agnes.

Bundled against the cold we walked the nearly two miles up over the hill and through the crusted fields, the three of us holding hands as the moon guided our way. After visiting, we would again make our way home. With the late night air much colder, we would hurry along. As we approached our home, it didn't matter how cold we were, because that's when the real magic happened. For there, the three of us would stand peering in through the darkened window as our tinselled tree sparkled from the rays of moonlight that fell across the kitchen floor. Once inside, Daddy would light the lamp and stoke up the fire, then with the lamp turned low we would sit around the opened oven door warming our feet, still in awe of the beauty of our Christmas tree. On that special evening, I was always so thankful that Daddy had insisted that we hang the tinsel "the right way." After all the twinkling electric lights I've since placed on my own Christmas trees, none have ever compared.

My tinsel now comes in the form of silver rope. Mostly, the same rope I have been using since the early eighties when the children were small, we were operating a dairy farm and I no longer had time to hang the tinsel pieces one by one. But the rope is still sparkly, beautiful and wonderfully warm. The ribbon I purchase? It looks beautiful as well, tied around lights, candles and wreathes. But it just doesn't hold the sparkle and magic of the tinsel. And on a moonlit Christmas night, when I turn off the electric lights and sit quietly by the tree, I'm sure I can feel the nip of frost on noses pressed against a cold window pane, hear the crunch of the snow beneath our feet and Daddy saying, "You're not finished yet girls, don't put that tinsel away, I see where you've missed a spot!"

The Chance Meeting

DAVID BETTS

OUR LITTLE HOUSE in Halifax always seemed so bare and dreary every Christmas Eve when my brothers and I were growing up in the 1940s.

When we went to bed around eight o'clock there were no Christmas decorations to be seen, no lights, no tree, no tinsel. And we didn't have festive Christmas stockings in those days, just dark blue and green Boy Scout socks to hang on the naked mantelpiece.

But we came downstairs on Christmas mornings to a wonderland! A fire blazing in the hearth; stockings stuffed with toys and goodies; colouring books and crayons, nuts and chocolates; a ceiling-high Christmas tree in the corner ablaze with lights; the sweet smell of spruce; and the sound of bacon sizzling in the kitchen.

It was the practice of Mum and Dad in our childhood years to wait until we were asleep on Christmas Eve before even beginning to decorate the house. When we were young boys we took for granted this annual Christmas "surprise," though looking back in later years I wondered, and wonder still, how our busy parents had the time and energy to carry out this delightful late-night ritual for our benefit.

In the week before Christmas our Dad would bring home a fresh, "wild" Christmas tree—always a spruce—he had cut from woods somewhere in Pictou or Cumberland Counties, which were part of his working territory as a civil engineer. One particular year he found two trees of almost equal merit, each being a near-perfect shape and having dense branches. Not able to choose between them, he put both on the roof of our old Pontiac and drove them to Halifax for the family to decide. After some hemming and hawing, mother and boys chose the one to be earmarked as the "surprise" Christmas morning tree. This was put in the garage, and the reject was left in the snowy back yard.

After we were in bed that Christmas Eve, our parents worked hard and late decorating the tree, filling our Scout stockings, wrapping and placing presents on and around the tree, affixing spruce boughs over doorways and through the stair spindles, festooning the hall and living room with ornaments, stuffing the chicken (we couldn't afford turkey) and cleaning and tidying every inch of the house.

As she slumped exhausted with a cup of tea around eleven P.M. Mum espied one more small object which she felt needed attention—a stamped and addressed envelope lying on a table beside the front door. As she later recounted, this was a routine piece of mail of no great urgency or importance, which could well have been left there for days, but it offended Mum's sense of tidiness and completeness, so she put on her coat and overshoes and trudged along the snowy sidewalk to put it in the mailbox at the corner, even though she knew it would not be picked up for two or three days.

In the hushed-late evening Halifax streets, it seemed no one else was stirring, but as she headed back home a neighbour about ten houses down from our place opened her front door to let her cat in.

My mother called out: "Merry Christmas, Mrs. Fuller!" (In those days my parent's generation almost always used surnames; only family and very close friends used first names.)

"Oh…hello, Mrs. Betts…I wish it were merrier," came the hesitant reply. Mrs. Fuller, normally a cheerful and outgoing person, seemed unhappy.

My mother paused. "Is anything the matter?"

"Oh, I'm sorry to be dreary," said Mrs Fuller. "It's just that our little Harry has gone to bed crying because we have no Christmas tree this year. My husband has been sick, you see, and I can't drive, so it was only late this afternoon that I got a chance to start walking around the streets trying to buy a tree, but everyone was sold out or had shut down for Christmas."

"Your problem is solved," Mum said cheerily. "We have an extra tree to which you are most welcome!"

Mrs. Fuller's face lit up. The two women dragged the spare tree down the street and into the Fuller house, where they spent until midnight decorating it and putting on strings of lights.

When six-year-old Harry Fuller came downstairs the next morning he had a REAL Christmas tree surprise, even better than the pretend ones my brothers and I enjoyed each year. To her dying day Mum could never fully explain what urge had impelled her to go out and mail an unimportant letter so late that chilly Christmas Eve. But little Harry was so glad she did!

Christmas Toys and Santa Claus

Seeing Santa, usually up close at the local department store, figures highly on a child's wish list, for Santa is the one credited with filling stockings and bringing toys on Christmas Day. As a result, many children fight to stay awake on Christmas Eve hoping to catch a glimpse of Santa's red suit. In the early 1900s when former New Brunswick resident Lester Tate was small, he made the mistake of sneaking out of bed to catch a glimpse of the jolly old elf. Unfortunately, the only person he saw leaving presents was an 'elfette' wearing his mother's apron. He had broken the household rule of not getting out of bed until he was called on Christmas morning and, as a result, Santa left no presents and Lester had to wait for his toys until the following year.

As in other places around the world, Maritime children practice the tradition of leaving cookies out to ward off the paunchy Santa's hunger as he makes his marathon trip around the world. Although the children may wish to share a cookie with him, most have to content themselves with receiving a note thanking them for their thoughtful snack.

Seeing Santa

JAMIE BRADLEY

I DON'T REMEMBER when I stopped believing in Santa Claus; perhaps my mind erased that moment to avoid the massive psychological trauma of harsh reality.

My eldest daughter, Melissa, had a smooth transition to the innocence-killing Age of Reason; honestly, my wife and I got off easy with that one.

With consumerism and advertising the successful sciences that they are, it's more difficult for parents to maintain the Santa magic when television commercials bleat their stocking-stuffer ideas.

"Um, well…" said Panicky Parent, "Santa only has about thirteen workshop elves helping him make presents and… the stores want him to know that…he can buy some things for our stockings at their store. Yes! These commercials are aimed at the North Pole and we're just accidentally receiving them!"

Whew!

My son Josh was six when the level-eyed demon reared its ugly, logical head. It all started as soon as the mall Christmas decorations came out, the day after Halloween, and the first images of the big guy emerged from the packing boxes. I noticed that Josh was looking a little more furtive than usual.

Josh asked me without looking up, "Daddy is there really a Santa Claus?"

I got panicky. But then it came to me; the smartest thing I ever could have said as a father: "Uh, what do you think?"

"I don't know."

"Hmm...I think there is." And then I proceeded to spout off anything my brain could latch on to support the theory of the creature known as Santaclausicus arcticus: "Yes Virginia," *T'was the Night Before Christmas*, Grinch, Frosty, A Child's Christmas in Wales (although it never mentions Santa and my Welsh accent is indecipherable even to the Welsh). I gave him a lot of confusing things to sort through, which only bought me time before facing the inevitable.

When I was six I had it all figured out, Santa Science:

Q   How come you see Santa at Eaton's and then you go across Mumford Road to Simpson's and he's there, too?

A   Come on, he can zip around the world, deliver presents (or coal), eat a million cookies, drink a million gallons of milk and get back to the North Pole for breakfast! In one night! Hopping around Halifax was nothing. That's why he took breaks.

Q   Why did Santa wear different suits while in different department stores and shopping malls?

A   Simple, Santa is fat and wears a wool suit with fur trim in a heated department store. Fat people sweat a lot so he has to change suits a lot. (Insert a cavalier laugh.)

But deep down, little Jamie had the same fear as his future son, Josh...Santa was a lie.

The season soon filled our lives and secret present caches. It was about five days before Christmas Eve when we happened to be strolling through a shopping mall looking for that perfect present for my wife because I always wait until the last week and just buy up what's left.

We strolled through the packed mall. At least it was safer to be inside the mall than in the parking lot. Somehow, mall parking lots seem to be Christmas-spirit-free zones. The magic cannot penetrate the frantic bubble of the yuletide demolition derby arena as furious drivers all vie for that one spot by the door.

Shoppers beetled in and out of stores and, dazed by decorations, I wondered what would happen if one of those oversized silver ornaments with the spear-like points fell from the ceiling. Would it imbed itself into the tile floor like a jackknife in a picnic table?

I suddenly felt my son's grip get tighter and we stopped dead in the middle of the flow. We were bumped from behind by a woman on a mission to find more intelligent toys for her child so the toy could play while the kid watched.

Josh was gazing at the silver and white decorated tree, well, Santa's throne...okay, Santa himself.

He took in a deep breath and said with wavering finality, "I don't think Santa Claus is real."

My heart sank and there was a long silence, which I'm sure was agony for my boy. Josh was only six years old, far too young to stop believing in anything. In school he wasn't even in a grade that had a number yet, for gosh sakes. It just wasn't time.

He was your typical mall Santa wearing the standard regalia of the office, a real beard, this one. I then realized that it was Santa who had to save himself from becoming mortal in my son's eyes.

I turned to Josh and saw in his eyes the mature preparation to accept the biggest disappointment in his young life. My dad will tell me the truth and it's going to hurt but I can take it.

"Josh, have we been in this mall before?"

His brow furrowed a bit. "No."

"Have you seen me talk to or signal Santa in any way?"

"No, Dad."

"And Santa is supposed to be magic and know everybody's name, right?"

Josh eyed the Claus, "Supposed to be."

I took a deep breath and put my faith in the legend. I waved to Santa and called, "Merry Christmas, Santa."

The Red Man looked up and called back, "Jamie, my goodness, how are you? My goodness, how you've grown!"

Josh's face turned the colour of Rudolph's nose and he burrowed himself under my coat until I finished chatting with my hero. I've since told John about his excellent performance. He's a great Santa.

Since that amazing day my entire family has managed to maintain an existence blissfully unaware of harsh reality and to pleasantly embrace blind belief.

Now there's just little Jennie to go.

The Longest-Serving Santa

BRUCE NUNN

(from *More History with a Twist,* Nimbus 2001)

ON A SNOWY CHRISTMAS MORNING in 1912, in a tiny Digby County village, a Christmas miracle occurred. Willis Tibbetts, an energetic farmer, lumberman, and handyman was up early that bright holy day morning, shovelling the Christmas Eve snow from his walk. Taken by the spirit of the season, he was moved to also clear his next-door neighbours' walk. The neighbours' children awoke later and immediately thought the snowy path out front had been magically created by Santa Claus.

Their innocent imaginations touched Willis and transformed his life forever. He decided then and there he would become Father Christmas for all the children of the twin villages of Brighton and Barton, near the head of St. Mary's Bay. And that he did, every Christmas Eve for sixty years. Right up into his nineties! Old Santa himself would be impressed.

Life had never been easy for Willis. Born into rural poverty in 1881, Willis was an infant when his mother died; he was raised by another family. With little education, he worked his way to New England, eventually becoming a faithful officer in the Salvation Army. He returned to Nova Scotia to work the land and care for an injured brother. He went to school as an adult, learned to read, and began a life of service to local children. A committed Salvationist, Willis married a Sally Ann officer in Digby who was claimed by illness within a few years. He was left with no mother for his children, yet he kept on giving to his community. Willis served as YPSM, the Young People's Sergeant Major. He treated kids to picnics on his land in summer. But each December 24, his mission was to do Santa's work.

The white beard was a given. At first it was a simple stringy thing. He fashioned a belt of bells to strap round his pillowed belly, cinching his red Santa suit tight. A wiry, muscled labourer, he wasn't quite the right build. But anyway, his heart was in it. Oh boy, was it ever!

Sure, he did the usual Christmas concert appearances for the Sally Ann and other denominations. Even into his fifties, this jolly fit elf would appear suited on stage doing a summersault to the children's delight. Into his eighties he would ride his bike the seven miles into Digby. But Willis Tibbetts's Christmas Eve home visits were the most special.

There's a Santa in every mall these days. But back then, back there, a Santa at your door brought your young imagination to life. Nola Jeffrey remembers the magic. In 1940 she was a young believer. Her Christmas memories of those magical moments in tiny Brighton are still brushed in her mind like an impressionist painting: fuzzy edged, but brilliantly bright in spots. The images of Santa swirl with the joy, the sounds and the smells of her childhood Christmas.

Nola is a retired teacher who hasn't lived in Brighton in decades. But she pulled back the curtain of time on her old painting of memories and let me peek into the past.

Imagine: it's Christmas Eve and five-year-old Nola is excited. She's been waiting all evening, and her mother has fresh-baked cookies cooling. Oh, the sound of jingling bells outside. A knock at the kitchen door. It blows open to a blustery whoosh of snow, and there he is. A tall, jolly, white-bearded Santa in his red suit. The bells are jingling. He's ho-ho-hoing. And young Nola's eyes are wide in amazement. Santa is in her kitchen!

"You would almost expect he had the reindeer waiting right outside," she told me.

Each Christmas Eve, Willis Tibbetts visited every child's house in the Brighton/Barton area. "He would laugh and talk and give us candy," said Nola.

Sometimes he gave small toys contributed by local folk. Then he'd move on. He covered about fifty houses in one evening. He did that every year for six decades, from 1912 up to 1972, stopping only a few years before he passed away at age 94. If you ask me, Willis was Santa Claus. He captured the spirit.

Generations of Brighton and Barton children knew Willis Tibbetts as "Santa Claus." That's who he was to them. His son Francis, now living in Eastern Passage, is happy to let his father's Santa story be told. It's a unique record: the longest serving Sally Ann Santa, perhaps anywhere.

Francis keeps his Dad's memory alive by keeping some old photos of his father as Father Christmas. That's not all he keeps. As we spoke, he gave his father's old Santa bells a shake on their worn leather harness. The nostalgic jingle-jingle of the bells had an instant emotional effect. Such a sweet, sweet sound. I imagined I was five and I shivered.

Merry Christmas.

The Teddy Bear

ROGER CYR

ONE OF MY MOST CHERISHED MEMORIES of Christmas is of receiving a wished-for toy, but it was not until Mother's Day of 1973 that I thought of it again. My Uncle Bob and I were planting trees along where the old barn used to sit and he said, "This is about the spot where I gave you the teddy bear on my last trip to sea." Those words, at that particular time, started a tape recorder playing in my head and the whole story replayed for me. I was overcome with emotion and it was like I had been transported back in time and I was a poor little kid again living in poverty on that old farm. When I lived there I had always looked forward to the day when I could get away and now there was no other place I'd rather be.

I stood under the maple trees that grew near the road and watched a figure walking towards our house. It was December and as he turned up the path that led to our back door I could see little balls of snow that clung to his heavy wool pants sparkling in the late afternoon sun. It was during the Great Depression of the 1930s, and my Uncle Bob was returning from a trip aboard the *Minas Queen* out of Parrsboro. To help support our family, he regularly sailed aboard one of the many ships that plied the coastal waters of Nova Scotia and beyond. North Atlantic storms had delayed their departure for England and made for a slow crossing with lumber from the local sawmills. The return voyage took them to Jamaica where they loaded casks of rum for the Boston market as prohibition had recently ended in the USA. Here the ship tied up for the winter, the crew paid and released to make their way back to Nova Scotia by train for Christmas.

As he drew closer, I moved back in the yard towards the barn until I was at a safe distance. He carried a duffel bag slung over his left shoulder and was holding a brown paper bag in his right hand. I wanted to run to the house and hide behind my grandmother, who I could see looking out the kitchen window, but he stood between safety and me. I had no memory of this person but he called me by name and took a small teddy bear from the paper bag and handed it to me.

I do not remember him speaking of other trips and I think that this was one of his favourite stories because of the teddy bear. He told it every time my mother came from Truro to visit. I don't think she ever grew tired of hearing it.

The teddy bear became my constant companion and I carried him everywhere for two or three years until his eyes and nose fell off. My grandmother sewed on a black button for a nose and two white beads for eyes. I started school in 1938 and soon forgot about the teddy bear.

When I was nine or ten years old I found teddy asleep in the closet under the stairway. He looked tattered and threadbare but the button nose and eyes were still intact. My grandmother had sewed his arms and legs back on and stored him away for safekeeping. Perhaps she intended for me to have him as a memento of my childhood. I carried the bear outside to a spot near where he was first placed in my hands and dug a hole in the ground. I placed the bear in the shallow grave and covered him over. To me he was a living, breathing bear, the very first toy I remember having and he had died.

When I visit my old home in Cumberland County, I find the spot where I buried the bear and reflect on my journey through life. I know now that I should have kept him.

Christmas Toys That Plagued Our Parents

DAVID GOSS

THERE WERE TWO ITEMS that always seemed to be under the Goss Christmas tree on St. James Street overlooking Beatteay's Beach and the mouth of Saint John Harbour that certainly were a plague to our parents. I know my Uncle Barney and Aunt Gwen were behind one: the tin drum that always got hidden away on Christmas night and was not found again until spring when we could be sent out in the yard to bang them without inflicting pain on our parents. But as for the other—the dart guns or the cork-shooting rifles—I was never sure how we came to receive them until just before my dad died, when he called me aside one time and made a confession that made it clear.

"David," he whispered, "you know there was one Christmas when you boys didn't receive much in the way of toys, and I have always felt badly about that."

Surprised, I said, "Dad, I couldn't tell you when that was and I am sure Doug and George couldn't either."

"Well," Dad said, "it was the year you did not receive any dart guns and there was a lot of other stuff missing too."

Knowing he wanted to tell the story, I said, "Well, I don't remember that Christmas, so you better tell me what happened."

Dad said, "Your mother and I always put as much aside as we could so you could have a good Christmas, and then, on Christmas Eve, we would go over to Emerson Brothers on King Street and pick up as many toys as we could afford. They would have them on at half price that night, so we could do all right. But, one year, we got fooled, and they didn't have the half price sale and you guys didn't get much."

I still didn't remember a year when there wasn't plenty, but vaguely I did recall that the dart guns and cork-shooting rifles stopped coming. However, I did not think it was due to a lack of finances, but that Mom had finally convinced Dad that we were shooting too many of her ornaments off the tree.

Whenever one was smashed to smithereens, none of us would have any idea what had happened. I thought she'd finally got through to him about how we would shoot corks and darts at our little sister BJ when she came barging into the mid-house bedroom when we would be playing cowboys and Indians. My brothers' brass rail bed became our horses, and we would tie a few blankets over the top and bottom bed frames to act as saddles, and would be riding along and shooting at one another or at whoever was hiding behind the dresser or on top of the closet.

We warned BJ many times it was a boy's game, but she just wouldn't stay out of that room, so we figured she got what she deserved if she stepped into the line of fire. I know Mom saw it differently, and many a time our guns were confiscated. I suspect that year they did not arrive at all it was Mom's way of stopping the shooting of our sister as I would have known nothing about the lack of a sale at Emerson's; I certainly assured Dad that he had nothing to feel sorry about.

Since we had the conversation, I have been hoping Santa would bring me a dart gun just one more time. If he did, I wonder if my wife would miss an ornament or two as quickly as my mom did. And when my sister comes to visit, I could find out if she could duck darts as adeptly as she did fifty years ago.

The Christmas Secret

GARY L. SAUNDERS

(From: *September Christmas*, Breakwater Books 1992)

SIDNEY JUST TUMBLED INTO OUR LIVES. The week before Christmas we got this telephone call from a neighbour saying, "Our son has brought home a friend of your son's from Mount Allison University for the holidays—perhaps you could come and pick him up?" Of course we would. Any friend of our son's was welcome. "But maybe you should wait until the smaller children are in bed," my neighbour added mysteriously. This should have told me something. But I was preoccupied with other things. I remember absent-mindedly wondering where we would sleep this person. No doubt, thought I, he would share Second Son's room when he arrived home from university.

As it turned out, this guest would fill the whole house with his presence and make the coming week one of the

most suspenseful Christmas countdowns of our lives. For
Sidney proved to be youthful, handsome, gregarious and
popular, a Prince Edward Islander by birth, an Allisonian by
circumstance, and a prankster by instinct. It was only later
we discovered he was addicted to chocolate, fond of booze,
loved to chase cats and roosters, and had fleas. For Sidney
was a dog.

A Christmas puppy, in fact, with all that this implies—
warm, fuzzy, cuddly, friendly, stumpy tail wagging while
he piddles on your foot with excitement. Big brown eyes
and moist black nose. Ten weeks old and chewing on everything and anything to relieve the sting of new molars.
And, of course, the inevitable newspaper business—and the
business without benefit of newspapers and sometimes the
business without benefit of footwear along
the dark hallway in the small hours.

At first we balked, my wife and I.
"Why a dog now?" our eyes asked
helplessly as I returned from my er-
rand and opened my parka to reveal
his polar bear cub face. Sidney's face
looked up, holding wonder like a
cup. "Why *not* a dog now?" our
eyes answered. And that was that.

Except for one thing. How to
keep it from the little girls until
Christmas morning? "Impossible,"
I said. "For one thing, where will he
sleep? For another, what about his
barking?" But Beth had a plan. School
wouldn't be out for several days, so
daytime would be no problem. The
rest of the time he would have to stay
in somebody's room—with somebody
entertaining him when he wasn't asleep.
Who would that somebody be?

"Not me," said Eldest Son, home on a visit. "I'm not going to sleep with a dog." Would Youngest Son, 16, do it? He would! So it was arranged. As soon as Youngest Son got off the bus each day, he would head for the back room and puppy-sit until relieved by one of us. To drown out any barking, a radio or stereo was always to be playing-especially in that critical period between when the girls arrived at 2:30 and when he came home an hour later.

I still had my doubts. But somehow—perhaps because everyone loves a secret—it worked but every day was a continuous game of wits.

"Mom, why is everybody going to the back room so much?" said Joyce one evening. Joyce was seven and already nobody's fool.

"Oh, they're wrapping Christmas presents," said her mother. Which was partly true.

Christmas drew nearer, as it always does, but slowly, too slowly. Joyce had developed a powerful urge to enter that room. She had to be constantly watched. "Why can't I wrap presents in there too?" she wondered. We put her off with more excuses. And at this point we decided that, since she has been the most curious and was suffering the biggest run-around, Sidney would be officially hers.

One morning near the start of Christmas vacation, Amber, the second youngest, appeared with a look of wonderment on her face. "There's a puppy in the back room!" she stammered.

"Shhh!" I whispered. Hugging her close, I whispered The Secret in her ear, and admonished her not to tell her sister. The bus came and off they went, Amber still wide-eyed and Joyce none the wiser.

At last, at long last, it is Christmas Eve. On top of all the usual excitement and suspense there is this time-bomb ticking in the back room, this present which must remain wrapped in mystery for at least a few hours more. The tree is up and decorated, the cakes baked, the presents put under the tree. At last the little girls have gone to sleep; now everything is ready. The parents drop wearily into bed. The house sits silent in the snowy night.

Soon a light clicks on in the upstairs hall, followed by a patter of feet to our bedroom door. "Can we go downstairs now? To look at our stockings?"

"So soon?" we groan. "It's 4:30 A.M.—not bad, compared to some years we can recall. "Sure, go ahead. We'll be down a little later." Away they go. And we lie in bed and listen— gauging the moment for the Secret Gift. The older children are still asleep. We don't want them to miss it. Should we wake them?

There's no need; here come the little girls again, shaking and waking them, eager to open presents, anxious to see how we like their own gifts to us. The whole family stumbles downstairs, eight of us in all, and in the pre-dawn darkness we hunker under the lighted tree and start to open our gifts.

Now is the moment. We bring him out. Sidney licks faces—wades happily in the sea of noisy paper. Noses the lowest ornaments. Scratches one ear; plunks himself down to watch.

And we watch Joyce, the object of this week-long conspiracy. Does she squeal with delight? Does she throw her arms around him, cover him with kisses? No such thing. She studiously avoids him. For the rest of us this is maddening. Perhaps she knew all along? Perhaps she was so sure Santa would bring a puppy that it's no surprise? After all, it was she who in November had taped signs all over the house saying, "I WANT A DOG"—signs that we tried to ignore.

We needn't have worried. A few hours later, when the pressure is off, she lavishes on him all the attention a puppy could want.

Since then he has squirmed and wagged his way into all our hearts. He has grown into a handsome golden retriever/cocker spaniel with the gentlest of dispositions and the greatest sense of humour. Sometimes we wonder how we did without him. Certainly Christmas at our house will need him from now on. Where other Yuletide gifts have worn out or vanished, our Christmas dog is running strong.

Toyland

AUDREY E. STRAIGHT

"TOYLAND, TOYLAND, EVERY GIRL AND BOY LAND!" This line from a Christmas song for children brings back memories of my childhood, of visiting the uptown stores in Saint John that prepared great toylands. MRA's on King Street also provided a Santa Claus sitting in his house or on his sleigh. There was always a large stream of children going to the top floor to visit the display of toys and talk to him and sit on his knee.

Also on King Street, Scovil Brothers provided a Santa Claus for visitation. Long lines formed on South Market Street some-

times even around the corner onto Charlotte Street. The other store was Duvals on Waterloo Street which had a great arrangement of toys upstairs over the hardware department. To reach Toyland, you went part way up on a central staircase, then branched off to the right or left to continue the rest of the way. Some of the children would make two trips due to the double set of upper stairs to Toyland.

In later years, Calp's store on Charlotte Street had a mechanical tricycle in their Christmas window on which a Santa sat and rode continuously night and day. Passers-by, both children and adults, watched with eager eyes. This was one of the first such displays, although the other stores mentioned also had attractive window displays. Once we saw the Christmas displays and Santa, we knew that Christmas was near. What excitement!

Santa's Mistake

CHARLES THOMPSON

THE SNOW BEGAN TO FALL just after supper. Like one of those Christmas ornaments you shake, it fell in large flakes and quickly began to build up. It was Christmas Eve 1969 and my sister and I decided to walk down the road to extend season greetings to our neighbours. When we arrived, the house was alive with family and friends. A party was in full effect despite the snow falling outside.

Over drinks and food the night passed quickly. Before we knew it, it was well past midnight. Realizing we had our five year old at home who would be up at first light, we began the long trek home. Even though the West Middle River Road had been newly paved, the ploughs had not yet put in an appearance. By now the snow was almost up to our waists. Filled with the spirit of Christmas, we laughed as

we pushed our way through the snow before finally climb-
ing the driveway to our home sitting high on a hill at the
base of the Cape Breton Highlands.

The house was in darkness as everyone retired to bed.

Just as we were about to tumble into our respective beds
my sister remembered she had bought a "Hot Wheels" set
that had to be assembled in time for the expectant child
on Christmas morning. We staggered into the living room
and began the arduous task of putting together this elabo-
rate set of tracks and cars before her son rose in a few short
hours.

Never a handyman, I was further impeded by much
good Christmas cheer at the recently departed neighbour's
house. We worked feverously, if somewhat clumsily, trying
to fit everything together.

Finally, just before the sun began its ascent over the
Highland range, we were done. Everything looked ready
for the big morning.

We flung ourselves down on the couches nearby and
grabbed what seemed like very few minutes of sleep before
excited squeals greeted us from upstairs. Our parents arose
and, along with my young nephew, descended the stairs to
see what Santa had brought.

My young nephew ran immediately to the freshly assembled Hot Wheels set. His face was aglow with the joy
of Christmas and the excitement at Santa's grand gift. My
dad reached down and handed him a car to try out the new
track. He carefully placed the car on the track and stepped
back to watch the little car race around the oval.

The car went a few inches and fell harmlessly to the floor.
His disappointment was obvious as his face fell like a cake
when the oven door slams. He tried again and the same
thing happened; the little car moved a scant few inches and
fell to the carpet. He was crushed. There was no consoling
him in his grief. Nervous glances were exchanged but no
answers were forthcoming to ease his pain.

My sister shot me an anxious look as if to say, "What's wrong?" By now the celebration that had taken place all night down the road was resulting in a huge headache and the pain was exaggerated by my failure.

I hoped against hope and reached down to try my luck. The same result: the car moved but a few short inches and once again fell to the carpet, its little wheels spinning sadly in the air. What had gone wrong in the late night?

As we all bent over the uncooperative car track I realized with a sudden rush of anxiety that I had worked into the wee small hours of the morning only to discover I had assembled the whole thing upside down. It was too late to fix my mistake. It would take hours to correct my errant ways.

My nephew was inconsolable. "Uncle Chuck, what's wrong?"

Despite my weakened mental condition, I immediately came up with an answer I hoped would get us through the morning with minimal damage.

"Well, Sandy, I explained, this is the first year for Hot Wheels (and it was) and Santa in his hurry to reach all the little boys and girls around the world must have installed it upside down by mistake. However he did leave the instructions behind so Uncle Chuck will put it right, OK?" Even at his young age, he realized he had little choice.

Well, justice aided by a couple of aspirins did prevail. The set was righted, the day progressed and after a lengthy delay one little boy had the unequalled joy of Christmas. It just took a little longer than either Santa or his Middle River helpers had anticipated.

The Christmas I Cried

LORETTA MACKINNON

FIFTY YEARS AGO, just a week before Christmas, at the tender age of six years, I was told by my best friend Valerie there was no Santa Claus. Her brother had told her and he should know because he was ten. That evening I told my parents and siblings what I had learned and I kept repeating it throughout the week.

Mom and Daddy kept telling me not to say there is no Santa Claus, because Santa may hear me, but I insisted I knew the truth. Nevertheless, I hung my stocking from the mantel just like the others. So Christmas morning we all bounded downstairs to grab our stockings and every one of them were bulging, mine included, but lo and behold, where theirs held an orange, grapes, nuts and candy mine held two onions, potatoes and a lump of coal.

To say I cried is an understatement. Shortly afterwards clumsy Mom "dropped" one of her new gloves behind the sofa so Daddy had to pull it out to get the glove. When he did, he found a big red felt stocking behind there, with my name on it, filled with all kinds of goodies. Daddy said, "It was probably Santa's way of showing me that he really does know if you've been good or bad." To be sure, I never repeated that nasty rumour about Santa again.

Toyland Memories

MILDRED GREGORY

ONCE THE SEASON WAS UPON US, the great excitement centred around the arrival of "Santa" at MRA's following the annual Christmas Parade. Santa was really Mr. Estey, manager of the Lower Price Department and he was a perfect Santa—medium height, quite rotund and very jovial. I was about eight years old and my mother took me to see Toyland and visit with Santa. Then came my great thrill. I approached Santa and he said, "Hello, Mildred, how are you, today?" He certainly made my day and left a memory I have always cherished.

At the age of ten, a best friend who was one year my senior informed me there was no Santa Claus. I was very upset and told my mother who assured me there certainly was a Santa. The days passed and when I awoke on Christmas morning my mother asked if I had seen what Santa had left on my pillow. There was a soft, white beardlike material that was actually a bit of cotton ball which had been stretched very thin. However, I was so excited I rushed to my friend's house and announced she was very wrong as I had the proof which I proudly produced. Santa had left me this piece of his whiskers to show he had been there!

Christmas Past

DONNA BUCKLEY

WHEN MY HUSBAND and I were dating back in the late '50s, I was invited to accompany his family in their traditional Christmas Eve adventure. This adventure consisted of my future father-in-law dressing as Santa, and visiting the homes of friends, family and business associates with small children. Arthur made a great Santa; just above the white beard and below the bushy white eyebrows, danced the bluest of blue eyes that any Santa would be proud to own. And even though some padding was added, not a whole lot was needed.

Santa and my husband would sit in the front seat, my mother-in-law and I would be relegated to the rear. All the windows would be rolled down and away we would go in a great flurry of noise and confusion. We would drive to the centre of town, and wave and yell "Merry Christmas" to any and all that we would see. I will always remember the man who had been celebrating the holidays very well, and very unsteadily, carrying his bottle in a brown paper bag, and bouncing off the buildings on one side and the parking metres on the other as he navigated the snowy sidewalk on King Street. Santa had us stop the car, and leaning out the window, jingling the bells as loud as he possibly could, and with even louder 'ho, ho, ho' he wished the man a Merry Christmas. As we drove away we could see the man looking at his bottle, looking at the retreating vehicle, and looking back at his bottle with a puzzled look. Tossing the bottle over his shoulder, he continued his unsteady way down the hilly street.

Santa didn't knock but would burst upon the scene, with his very loud 'ho, ho, ho' and ringing, jingling bells. He would admire the Christmas tree and tell the children to be good and go to bed so that he could bring them the rest of their presents.

As is the custom in Irish homes—and most of my father-in-laws friends were of Irish ancestry—Santa couldn't leave a home without some liquid refreshment, "To warm the innards on such a cold and snowy night." By the end of the evening, his 'ho, ho, ho' would be very enthusiastic. His red nose and cheeks would no longer be the result of rouge or the cold weather.

But all was not fun and games. A friend of the family was a grocer in a poor and rundown neighbourhood. He knew all the families and their incomes. He knew the ones who would and could provide a Christmas and Santa for their children. He also knew the families who would go without. My father-in-law and some of his business associates would collect toys, clothing and groceries to provide a Christmas for these proud families. They never knew where these goods came from or the name of the Santa who delivered them. For days after Christmas these families would come into the grocer's shop and tell him of the wonderful gifts they received.

It was tradition in our home, and in most of the homes of that era, that the Christmas tree was put up on Christmas Eve and trimmed after the children were in bed. This way the children were brought up believing that Santa trimmed the tree as well as brought the gifts. Santa was truly a busy and magical man indeed!

One year as we were on our way home and it was well past midnight, we passed a house with lights on and in the window we could see a young couple trimming a tree. Insisting that we stop the car, that children had to be present in that home, Santa jumped out, dashed up the stairs, and burst into the home of this unsuspecting couple. Watching through the window, we could see Santa shaking hands with a most bewildered young man, and hugging a very surprised young woman. Disappearing for a couple of minutes, we found out that Santa went into the children's bedroom, told them to go to sleep so he could come back and bring them their presents. Just as quickly as he arrived,

Santa left. This couple never found out who Santa was or why he visited them that night. But he did leave them with a very wonderful memory of a special Christmas Eve. And we never found out who they were either.

Then there was the year that we had a terrible snow storm, with blizzard and white-out conditions. The police were issuing warnings to stay off the roads, but not Arthur. He had promised these children that they were going to see Santa, and see him they would. He insisted that we stick to our schedule as there were a lot of children waiting for him. How could you explain to children Santa couldn't make it because it was snowing?

Arthur's car was a new model and very light in the back. Even chains didn't work for him. My dad had an older, heavier model and we borrowed his car. Dad neglected to tell us that he had been replacing the floor in the back and there was bare metal, with no carpeting or mats to cover it. My mother-in-law and I tried to quickly get into the back seat before Santa returned and our feet slid out from under us, and we found ourselves on our backs staring at the roof. I must admit that I got to know my mother-in-law very well that year.

My father-in-law's greatest hope was to be able to put the Christmas spirit back into this, the most wonderful, magical night of the year.

Santa Comes to Town

JOHN PAYZANT

DEPENDING ON YOUR LOCATION, Santa Claus appears in your fireplace on Christmas Eve, your department store in November, or in a motorized sleigh at the end of an enormous parade. But not here in Lunenburg!

I read in the local newspaper that St. Nick was expected downtown on the last Saturday in November. While strolling along the waterfront on a beautiful sunny day, I came upon a wharf crowded with children and parents, buzzing with anticipation. At precisely 1:00 P.M., a vessel appeared on the horizon steaming into Lunenburg's beautiful little harbour. At the same time, a bright yellow fire truck started backing onto the wharf causing little faces to turn their attention away from the sea. When the truck came to a stop, all eyes turned seaward to spot a fishing boat heading purposefully towards the dock. As the boat got closer, a large Christmas tree could be seen sprouting from its bow. The 150-ton fishing trawler *M/V Cape Keltic* started to slow and Santa emerged from the bridge waving vigorously at the crowd. The kids squealed with excitement and crowded to the edge of the dock as the boat pulled along side. When the crew had it securely tied, Santa started to climb down a steel ladder running from the bridge to the deck. Sadly, his ample paunch was in the way so some crew-members pushed him back up and he disappeared into the wheelhouse only to reappear on the deck from a doorway below. He then jumped ashore and ho-ho'd with the little ones gathered around. After a while, he tottered over to the fire truck and climbed aboard as it inched its way off the wharf. Santa was last seen waving at everyone from the back of the truck as it drove away.

Some sleigh! Some chimney!

The Waiting

SEAN FLINN

AFTER MIDNIGHT MASS, the little boy left the church, rushing out ahead of his parents and most of the other parishioners.

At the top of the broad steps, he circled the concrete pillars, running his hand along the surface of each one. His parents came out wishing friends Merry Christmas.

The little boy walked between his parents. They left the steps of St. Thomas Aquinas hand in hand to cross Oxford Street on Jubilee Road. Snowflakes fell as big as the paper ones he folded and cut out at school—big snowflakes that floated far apart, as if respecting each other's need for space.

The little boy's mother, a piano teacher, admired the thick front doors hung with pine cones and little gold metal balls that rung when the door opened to welcome guests, revealing the music and warmth within. The father, a carpenter, admired the houses' solid framing, the grain of the wooden doors and the trim around windows. The little boy chattered along Jubilee Road. His father smiled down at the boy, whose toque was weighed over by the pom-pom. The little boy talked into the cold night air about the gifts lying in wait underneath the colourful paper, about the calls from relatives. On Connaught Avenue, the little boy halted and announced, "I hate waiting for Christmas."

"Sweetie, Christmas is no time for hate," the little boy's mother said, gently tugging him along.

After a short silence, the little boy launched his lament again. His parents looked at each other knowingly over top of him. They'd heard this complaint many times before and they agreed their son felt weighed under by anticipation, waiting for the decisive moment to take action. Sometimes they worried about him, knowing the world demanded quick decisions, actions to be taken. The little boy must learn to carry the weight. His parents agreed to talk to his teachers over the coming new year.

They crossed Quinpool Road over to Newton Avenue. They turned on to First Street and saw the white points of light outlining their little house's windows. It was tiny, like the houses in a Monopoly game. A saltbox house, the boy's father had knocked down walls, refinished floors and the basement for the boy to play in. The little boy asked if he could open a gift tonight. "I can't wait," he pleaded, "Just one."

His parents expected this. Earlier they agreed they would give him the new baseball glove. It was the right choice: their son would have to wait months before spring came and he could use it. His appetite satisfied and his interest in such a gift not too strong, they concluded that he'd sleep.

The little boy went up to bed after 2:00 A.M. after his mother told him Christmas morning would arrive in no time. Following a couple of books read with his father lying back against a pillow, all was quiet. The little boy's parents murmured softly to each other, and placed the last few gifts under the tree.

Then they heard it: the little boy threw up. His mother rushed upstairs, telling him, "It's alright sweetie, it's all right. It's over now." While she changed him into new pyjamas and pulled the sheets off his bed, she sent the boy downstairs to sit with his father.

"Hi fella, your tummy not well? It's probably just nerves." His father said, the boy sitting on his lap. The little boy's father knew the expectancy of the evening was too much for his son.

"Let's look at your new glove," the little boy's father said, reaching over from his rocking chair to pick up the glove. The little boy slid it on his left hand, staring absently down at it. The father grinned at the sight of his son in fresh blue pyjamas wearing the big, brown leather glove.

The father rubbed his boy's back with one broad, thick hand and laid the other flat against his chest, as if to steady his son. "It's just nerves," the father repeated. The little boy felt soothed by his father's patience and his strong hands. He was "a carpenter, like Jesus and his father Joseph," the little boy's teacher told him during an Advent celebration.

"All set honey," the little boy's mother called from the top of the stairs.

"Good night, Dad," the little boy said, pale and vacant.

He hugged his father around the neck.

"Merry Christmas, son."

He watched the little boy climb the stairs, the glove still on his hand. Why did he choose baseball, the father wondered, alone for a moment. Baseball was a game of waiting: the pitch, the swing, the play. He watched his son play. His son was good, the coach said, and could get better. "Don't wait to get him into training."

During games, the father froze the moment when the white, blurred orb hung in the air between the thrower's descending hand and his son's outstretched glove. The father tried to imagine what his son thought during this brief moment in time, whether his head was full of tumult or clear with purpose. His boy always caught the ball with a snap of his glove. The father always felt relief. His boy was good, his boy would be fine. Now, on Christmas Eve, he couldn't wait to watch his son play again this spring.

Christmas Miracles and Gifts

hether it is a simple donation of food brought to a hungry family or a specially chosen present for a dear friend, part of the excitement of the season is planning to surprise people you love with a gift. Maritimers are known for their generosity and so it is no real surprise that some of the most tender stories of the season centre around the giving and receiving of gifts. One mother was determined to hide her son's present until the proper time on Christmas morning but she despaired when she saw her son had accompanied her husband to pick her up from the mall after her shopping spree. She quickly hid her present and hobbled, stiff-legged, to the back seat of the car. Her son believed she had had a fall but he was amazed at her quick recovery when he saw her walking with no limp on Christmas morning. Most likely the unusually quick healing had something to do with the hockey stick Santa left behind.

When You Give From the Heart

ANNE-MARIE CAISSIE

LOUISE SCROUNGED through her freezer, pushing everything aside to retrieve the turkey hidden far below. She hoisted up the heavy bird, carried it up the stairs, and plunked it on the counter. Down the stairs she went again, directly to the cold room where the vegetables were stored for the winter. Louise managed to balance the bag of potatoes and carrots in her arms, while she plopped the squash on top. Taking precaution, she manoeuvred her way up the stairs and into the kitchen.

A woman on a mission, you might say. Louise's knees creaked like old wooden steps as she crouched down to peer inside the Lazy Susan where she kept her canned goods. Out came the cranberry sauce, along with cans of peas and corn. Her mind visually captured the scene of her table adorned with the Christmas feast, just moments before her family would say the blessing.

"Dressing," she said aloud. She jerked the cupboard door open and grabbed a box of Stuff n Such. Her sweet tooth reminded her that apple and pumpkin pies were in the fridge. A bag of freshly baked homemade rolls was nestled on top of the breadbox.

Louise was satisfied; she now had everything that she planned to serve for her Christmas dinner.

Snowflakes lightly kissed her cheeks as she lugged the array of food out to her car. Arriving at her destination, Louise was grateful: there was available parking right near the entrance to the food bank. Just as she opened the trunk, a little old man with a friendly face approached her and said, "Need any help carrying that stuff inside?"

"Yes," she said. "That would be appreciated."

Louise chatted with the attendant inside the food bank. "This is very nice of you," he said.

"You're welcome," she replied with a smile. She turned around and headed for the door, then stopped. Something else needed to be done. Louise walked back toward the counter and opened her purse. She grabbed her wallet and emptied its contents; bills and coin scattered everywhere on the countertop. A quick calculation indicated fifty dollars and sixty-two cents. "Here," she said to the attendant. "Money will be needed to buy gas, to deliver the food boxes."

On the drive home she thought of her family's reaction to having no traditional Christmas dinner. She laughed as she pictured their shocked faces when she broke the news. Especially the youngest child; pumpkin pie was her favourite dessert.

CHRISTMAS BLESSINGS

Louise's heart was happy that someone else would enjoy a Christmas dinner. Her family shared many holiday celebrations together and hopefully would, many more. Money in her house was in short supply, so she could not easily replace what she had donated. Louise didn't care. She would be creative and serve something different for her family.

The next day was Christmas Eve. Louise was excited as she bustled around the house, putting finishing touches on her Christmas decorating. Her husband, Darryl, arrived home from work early in the afternoon.

Looking at the clock perched above the stove, she asked, "How come you're home so early?"

Darryl appeared very anxious. "I have surprise for you," he said.

"You do. What is it?"

Darryl slid his hand inside his jacket pocket, pulled out an envelope and handed it to her. "Apparently the company had a very productive year and decided to give the employees a five-hundred-dollar Christmas bonus."

"You've got to be kidding," she said. "You haven't received a Christmas bonus in years."

"I know," said Darryl. "Isn't this wonderful news?"

Louise could not believe their good fortune. It was then that she realized what she always knew to be true. When you give from the heart, you will receive back when you least expect it.

She looked at the clock and glanced at the cheque in her hand. There was still time to run to the bank, make a deposit, and get to the grocery store before it closed to re-buy everything that she had given away. Louise was just about to step outside, but instead stood still for a moment. She truly felt that Christmas was not about turkey and all the fixings; it was about giving and celebrating the birth of Jesus.

Louise decided to keep her secret to herself. She went back into the kitchen and went about her business of mak-

6

ing seafood chowder. Serving it on Christmas Eve was a tradition in her family, one that she would honour.

The Very White Christmas

BUDGE WILSON

(from *Winter Welcomes*, Ed. John McInnes, Clayton Graves, Christine McClymont)

MOST PEOPLE in the little Nova Scotia village thought it was going to be a green Christmas, but they were wrong. When the big soft flakes of snow began to fall on December 22nd, everyone was pleased, even the grown-ups.

Down at Dupont's Beach, Marc Comeau was sitting on a rock. He held his face up to the sky and let the cold snow tickle his throat. Then he looked at the snow flakes gathering on his coat sleeve, bringing his arm close up to his face so that he could see them clearly. The flakes were like stars, and every star was different.

When his friend Mariette found him staring at his sleeve, she laughed and laughed. "Now I've seen everything!" she hooted, slapping her knees. "Boats and islands in front of you and waves breaking. And what do you look at? Your arm!" Then Marc showed her the stars, and soon they were both watching their sleeves.

But the snowstorm wasn't a happy thing for very long. By noon, the wind had risen. The snow swirled past the windows and piled up on the sills till you couldn't see outside. Everyone stayed indoors, even the fishermen—as soon as they had tied their large boats to the Government Wharf, and hauled the small ones up onto the land.

By nightfall, you couldn't even tell where the road was. From his bedroom window, it looked to Marc as if someone had put the village in a white box and closed the lid. No one could get in or out. And the Weatherman said that the snow would continue for two more days. No roads would be open until at least Boxing Day

Marc was wild with worry. He had planned to go to Yarmouth on Christmas Eve to buy presents with the money he had earned on his paper route. Now he had nothing to give his mother or father. And nothing for Mariette, who was his very best friend. Of course he could make presents for his parents—who always liked whatever he made—but what can you make for a *girl*?

Marc picked up Diane, the family's big black cat, and cried into her fur. Then he lay face down on the bed, filled with gloom.

But there was worse to come. Soon after the Weatherman had delivered his terrible news over the radio, Madame Comeau came into the bedroom and put her hand on Marc's shoulder. "Mon petit chou," she said. "I have sad things to tell you. I have not bought you one single present for Christmas. Like you, I was leaving all my Christmas shopping until our trip to Yarmouth, and now we are stuck here like prisoners in a white jail. I'm so sorry."

Marc knew he had to say something, and he also knew he should try to make his mother feel better. But he couldn't think of what to say. If he said, "I don't care if I get any gifts," it would be a lie. So he just squeezed his mother's hand and said, "Try not to worry," which is exactly what his mother would have said to him.

On December 24th, the snow finally stopped falling, the wind went somewhere else, and the sunshine burst out from behind the dark clouds. The villagers came out of their houses like animals out of their holes, and started to stare, and to shovel, and to make snowmen, and to lie down in the snow to make angels. Marc was so excited that he forgot to be miserable for hours at a time. His mother told him it was the biggest snowstorm she had ever seen in her whole life, and she was thirty-three years old.

"Enjoy it!" she said. "You may never see snow like this again. It's sort of a Christmas gift from the Weatherman."

And almost everyone in the village did enjoy it. Mind you, old Uncle Bernard Cloutier made a terrible fuss about it, and refused to leave his house. His wife had to do all the shovelling, and even had to milk the cows and feed the chickens. But Uncle Bernard always complained about everything anyway—kids' noises, too much sun, too much rain, the Income tax, his lumbago, barking dogs, and his wife's piecrust. So no one paid any attention to him.

After lunch, Marc and Mariette made a little snow house up against the side of the Comeau's barn. They climbed all the way up to the roof of the chicken house and jumped off. They took a big stick over to Martel's Hill and wrote "Merry Christmas" and "Joyeux Noël" in the snow, in letters so big that you could see them from an airplane. They stood under an apple tree and shook it, making their own private snowstorm.

Even the grown-ups had fun. Marc's father dragged the old snowshoes and toboggan out of the woodshed, and took his wife for a long ride down in the back pasture. Madame Comeau pulled him all the way back.

That evening there was no church service, because no one could get to the big church at Pointe de l'Église. So everyone dug out as many candles as they could find—from their kitchen drawers and attics and bathroom cupboards—and gathered in the big field behind Mariette's home, where there was a giant spruce tree. Then they lit their candles and circled the tree. They walked slowly around it, singing carols in the snow. Marc thought he had never seen anything so beautiful.

On Christmas morning, Marc awoke, his mind full of memories of the day before. He lay in bed and let the pictures pass before his eyes—the snow house, the tobogganing, the carol-singing in the snow. He felt very warm and content, and almost forgot to think about presents. Then his mother came into the bedroom, her face lit up with delight and excitement.

"Quick!" she whispered to Marc. "Come quick! The family has just received a wonderful Christmas gift! Your father found it when he went downstairs to light the stove." She led the way to the kitchen. Mr. Comeau was there, waiting.

There in her basket by the big stove was Diane, black as night and purring loudly. And beside her, nuzzled up to her and very tiny, were four new kittens—three black and one grey.

"One each," said Marc's father. "One for me, one for your mother, and one for you. And, if you like, you may have one for Mariette."

Marc was so happy that he thought he might actually burst. But he didn't. Instead, he bent down to kiss Diane and to touch each kitten very gently, very tenderly. Pointing to the grey one, he said, "That one's for Mariette. Because it's special." Then he hugged his mother and his father, and laid his hand on Diane's beautiful head. "Merry Christmas everybody," he said.

Spread the Warmth

DEBORAH GRAHAM

"I'M SO THANKFUL!"

The relief in her voice was obvious as they pulled out of the parking lot and drove away from the city. Once they were on the highway headed towards Truro, Cathy reclined her seat and thought about what the doctor had said, "No evidence of MS!" Her symptoms, weakness and unrelenting fatigue, had been the result of some fluke virus. As they drove along, she looked over at her husband and said, "I'd like to do a little project."

"What kind of project?" he asked.

"I don't know, I just feel like I've been given a gift and I need to do something in return—something to help others."

"What can I do?" she wondered as her life settled back into a normal routine. One day as she and her daughter Mary were driving along the road, an idea began to take shape in her mind. She'd heard some youth were living in Victoria Park. Their reasons for leaving their homes were varied but they all had one thing in common—trying to sleep in the park at this time of year was impossible. It was cold! "I'd like to do something to help," Cathy said wistfully to her daughter.

"What's stopping you?" Mary replied.

For a moment Cathy was taken aback by her daughter's candid question. The more she thought about it, the more possibilities began to surface. With the cold nights they'd been having, she thought about blankets. Not just one or two blankets, but a lot of blankets. Even old blankets would do but secretly she hoped for some new ones too. Mary's question spurred her to action. "Let's call the project 'Spread the Warmth,'" her friend Nikki responded enthusiastically when Cathy shared her idea. She was delighted with Nikki's suggestion and, with Mary's help, she launched the campaign.

Mrs. Bradley and the "quilting ladies" from St. David's United Church on Pictou Road donated fourteen of their new quilts to the worthy cause. Through the generosity of the townspeople, approximately one hundred blankets were collected and distributed that first year.

News of the project spread quickly and by the time the next year rolled around, collection boxes were placed at a number of locations throughout the town. Before Christmas, Cathy and her helpers collected the blankets and took them to the local sharing club for distribution. As a result of her endeavours, Cathy became known as the blanket

angel. In the years since 1999 the townspeople have continued to make generous contributions to the cause and
the ladies from St. David's church have given more quilts
and recently have added warm hats and mittens to their
donations.

This December, Cathy and her team of volunteers plan
to combine the blanket campaign with an art show. The
underlying purpose in combining the two events is to cre-
ate more awareness of the growing need of reaching out to
others by spreading the warmth in their town. Each artist
has agreed to contribute a percentage of their sales to the
food bank. In keeping with the overall theme of sharing
and spreading the warmth, it is no coincidence that the art
will reflect warmth, kindness and helping hands.

What began as a humble endeavour seven years ago has
grown to surpass Cathy's dream. Each year more blankets
appear in the boxes. Now, hundreds of blankets are collected and given to those in need. Over the years, others have
offered their support by becoming actively involved in the
campaign. Wouldn't it be wonderful if we could help spread
a little warmth in our communities this Christmas?

Grandfather's Last Christmas

KELLY DOUGLAS

BY NOVEMBER of 1989 my grandfather, who had been ill
for several years, knew that it would be his last Christmas
and he wanted to do something special for each member
of his family. All his life he had been very careful with his
money. He repaired old radios for extra cash and bought
my grandmother's dishes with Texaco gas coupons. When
he repaired household items, he used what was available. I
later inherited his favourite chair and when I took it apart to

reupholster it, I discovered he had strung it with electrical wire instead of fabric webbing.

He wanted to do something special for each member of his family and as oldest granddaughter, the shopping fell to me as he was housebound and hated shopping. I carefully selected items and brought them to him for his approval and he reimbursed me. He got a fur coat for my grandmother, amethyst earrings for my mom, and jewellery for my sisters. Of course he had one gift left to get that I couldn't buy for him, mine. He asked me what I wanted and there really wasn't much I wanted or needed but I was recently divorced and my husband had gotten custody of the tools so I suggested he buy me a set of screwdrivers, a hammer and a saw.

My father told me later my grandfather insisted on going himself to select my gift so he took him shopping to Canadian Tire with oxygen tank in tow. It was the only time grandfather had been out of the house in months. On Christmas Day I opened a large tool chest filled with wrenches, screwdrivers, a hammer, pliers, saws (both regular and electric), a drill, and metal shears among other things. I was ready to set up a workshop.

A few years back, Canadian Tire came out with a Christmas village piece as a Canadian Tire store. My son bought it for me for Christmas to remind me of my grandfather and it is the best gift I have ever received.

Christmas Reflections

BLAKE MAYBANK

IT WAS A CALM DECEMBER DAY, a rare enough event in Nova Scotia, but the temperature was also ideal, a bit below freezing, making it easy to walk the nearby rough forest trail, its muddy sections firm underfoot, the wet sections frozen over. The sky was overcast, a uniform light-grey sheet, the colour of peeling tree bark. It took us less than an hour to reach our favourite lake even though we stopped periodically, once to listen to chickadees, another time spending several minutes to enjoy the deliberate movements of a black-backed woodpecker as it searched for insect eggs. The general silence was comforting, not unnerving, though there were occasional brief noises—odd popping noises from dead tree trunks, a distant "cronk" of a raven, a delicate tinkle where a tiny stream still flowed over icy rocks.

When we arrived at the lake we expected it to be ice-covered, but the area around the outlet stream was still open and the placid water, reflecting either the grey clouds or the bordering trees, was alternately light or dark. And because it was Christmas, the peaceful scene seemed amplified. The calm was both startling and soothing.

As we stood on the lakeshore the only sound was the dull rough-and-tumble of the stream, mixed with the gentle labour of our breathing. Without announcement it began to snow, a small flurry of scattered rotund flakes, heavy enough to force a direct path from sky to ground, untroubled by breezes. Each flake hit the water as if shot from a bow, and where the water reflected the clouds, the mirrored surface produced the illusion of each flake bouncing back skyward, matching the downward flakes in fortitude and speed. On a larger scale, with hundreds of flakes hitting the water like a trampoline, the effect was dizzying: snow rushing downward and skyward simultaneously, never colliding, a kaleidoscopic silent movie of small white balls bouncing on a grey marble floor.

I shifted my gaze slightly to where the snow fell on shadowed water, and against this dark backdrop the illusion abruptly changed. The flakes, though still reflected, now seemed to dive into the water instead of returning heavenward, and the speed of their descent seeming quite unnatural, as if they were still passing through air. The shadow flakes' dark descent measured against their neighbours' bright ascent caused further reflection within my secular soul.

As I continued to watch the rise and fall of the flakes, the tempo suddenly changed, many more flakes joining the frenzy. As the snowfall increased it became impossible to focus on any one particular flake, and the illusion became dispelled by the multitude; the reflective show was over. We suddenly noticed that our hands and feet were cold, reason enough to retrace our steps homeward, notwithstanding the show's finale. During our return stroll a few forest birds made their presence known; golden-crowned kinglets flitted on nearby firs like tiny tree ornaments, and a pileated woodpecker, with its crimson crest, seemed somewhat angelic perched near the top of a tree. Our last avian encounter was with a grouse (a partridge, to some), that rushed quickly off our path into thick bush, though not a pear tree could be seen. It was a reminder of our hunger; with our souls now full of seasonal spirit, our bodies needed the same.

No Big Deal

LEN WAGG

GROWING UP IN RURAL NOVA SCOTIA with farms all around, the dirt roads and the rolling landscapes made every Christmas almost Rockwellian in nature. I moved with my family to a place called North Kingston to an abandoned old-century farmhouse with a huge barn and numerous outbuildings. The house sat facing the North Mountain and when snow blanketed the fields it would bring images of deer running from the tree line and pristine, non-cow-patty-touched hills to toboggan on.

One Christmas Eve, my father and sisters left for town
to fetch my mother from work and pick up the Christmas
groceries, which meant goodies that were scarce during the
year would be abundant during the next few days.

I was home alone and kept watching nervously out the
kitchen window as the storm which started earlier in the
day worked itself up into a full-blown snowstorm and the
road began to fill quickly. As the wind came up, the house
would buckle and I could feel an occasional crack as a gust
hit it broadside after tumbling down the mountain.

The kitchen was warm, a haven with the huge beast of a
stove that burned wood from dawn to bedtime. The grumbling from the summer as my sisters and I had lined up and
handed each other the slab wood, stacking it in the woodshed until it touched the roof, only then to start another
row, was long gone.

Waking up in the morning, I would rush to the kitchen
knowing I could quickly heat up close to the stove. The tea
was started in the morning on the backburner and, as the
day went on, more water and more teabags were added to
the pot; the smell of tea was ever-present. Some days, the tea
pot would hold nine or ten bags and the only way to whiten
it would be with a good dose of Carnation milk and sugar.

When the stove was in full burn I would throw tea-
spoons of water across it when no one was around and
watch how much of a hiss it would make and how far the
bubbles would scurry. A bag of dulse, seaweed collected
from the shores of the Bay of Fundy, would become a treat
roasted on the heat of the iron.

As cosy as it was, I was getting nervous. My parents should
have been home by now and the snow was getting thicker.
With no streetlights on the dirt road, I waited for a sign of
headlights announcing their arrival. Then, it happened.

A loud "EEEEIIIIII" seemed to come from all over the
house yet from no room in particular. The eerie scream
drained all the blood from my face and washed a feeling of

dread over me. The dogs looked around and pushed themselves up to investigate.

I checked every room; the scream seemed to fade in and out. Arriving in the foyer, I knew the sound was coming from upstairs. I walked across the iron grate—once the source of heat for the house before a wood-burning stove in the dirt basement had given up its useful life.

I went upstairs. Although fading, the scream was constant. The sound came from the attic.

The attic door was in the upstairs bathroom. It was small and had a latch on it that jiggled and made noise when the wind blew. When I woke up in the middle of the night and could no longer hold the pressure in my bladder, I had noticed the attic door. At twelve years old, the attic is where the monsters live. It's the "Choky" in the movie *Matilda*, the door to Hades, the place where all those ten-minute clips from the series *Night Gallery* were born.

I lifted the latch, opened the door and walked up in the darkness to the top of the stairs. I reached the pull chain for the light, and as I did the noise stopped.

I looked around and made my way over to the noise. There, sitting between two joists, was a…mouse. He had been snapped in a mousetrap midriff and lasted long enough to make that horrible sound in the last few minutes of his life. Sitting beside him was the cold air return aluminium pipe that connected to the heating system of the house. The scream was amplified and sent around the entire house through the furnace heating system. One monster down.

I left and ran downstairs to keep up my vigil and get back to the warmth of the wood stove. Feeling a little silly and a little cocky at the same time, I threw some wood in the fire and watched for lights through the snow. Suddenly, the kitchen door blew open and for the second time that night it felt like my bowels would empty.

Standing in the doorway was my father, holding groceries bags that were soaked from the wet snow, spilling canned goods onto the kitchen floor. "Grab these," he yelled as I got some mobility back in my shocked system and moved forward. "We went off the road in the snow about a mile back." He left again to get another load as my mother and sisters made their way in, each wet and tired and trying to balance a soaked load of goodies. Soaked and tired they all came home and started to tell me about their night of making it home for Christmas.

The wood stove was stoked and wet clothes were hung all around. My mother asked if I was okay being home alone for that length of time and I remember telling her, "It was no big deal."

"Oh Little Town of Bethlehem" in St. Andrew's-by-the-Sea

PATRICIA ANNE ELFORD

THE PERFECTLY-SHAPED CHRISTMAS TREE, dressed in shimmering red and silver and white, breathes evergreen through the sanctuary. Albert, seated at the balcony Casavant organ, plays the first chord.

The Church School members, ranging from toddler to preteen, are robed in burgundy miniatures of adult choir gowns, their lightly-starched, white collars almost shining. They stand on the bottom steps of a steeply-curved staircase which rises to the precentor's[1] box, then circles on up to the second-story pulpit. Little faces glowing in tree and candlelight, the children joyfully, nervously, sing their chorus. After the singing, one tiny girl curls up in the minichoir's box pew and sleeps through the rest of the service. Similar scenes are being enacted in many churches, but for us, the clergy family, for this congregation, the event is very special.

There has been no full-time ministry here, no Sunday school, in St. Andrews-by-the-Sea, New Brunswick, for fifteen to seventeen years, just pulpit supply. In 1979, historic Greenock Presbyterian Church has been threatened with final closure.

The tiny Women's Missionary Society group stands firm, asking Presbytery for one more chance for this church to be a witness to God's present presence, rather than a museum of the elegant, dusty past. The small, determined congregation is ready, with God's help, to make it work.

Guided by the Mission Superintendent, W.J.O. Isaacs, a well-considered mission appointment—Rev. Robert J. Elford—is arranged for Greenock and Penfield churches. It is a very good match. The beautiful, big manse is reopened and prepared. At Christmas, this manse also has a Penfield-groomed Christmas tree in the curve of its staircase, sparkling with mini-lights and family decorations which have travelled safely from Ontario. A huge arrangement of fruit, a congregational gift, overwhelms the dining-room sideboard.

"There will be a Sunday school," says the new minister.

"But, we are an older congregation," replies one elder. "There are no children."

"We have our own family," says the minister. "They need Sunday school. That's a start. Have you no nieces and nephews, no grandchildren, no neighbours, who would attend here if a Sunday school were available?"

Sunday school begins, and within three years, there is also a vacation Bible school.

In the church hall, which has been winterized and improved, there is another perfectly-shaped, giant tree from the same Christmas tree farm in Penfield. It is so tall the children have to perch on chairs, blowing silver tinsel from funnelled hands to decorate its top branches. It, too, is dressed in white and silver and red. At its top is a natural star, a large "sand dollar."

The church is filled to its 500-seat capacity when the travelling Knox College choir presents a concert. (It doesn't hurt that half the normal school is cancelled so the elementary children can attend.) The famous summer sale has been joined by a Christmas sale and tea. There are evening and daytime Bible studies in both points of the charge.

Apparently feeling that their purpose is completed, several members of the tiny WMS (Women's Missionary Society) group die. The Ladies Guild and WMS become one. They join the rest of the congregation for this very special event, this Christmas Eve service.

Albert McQuaid, blind since infancy, has played the beautiful Greenock organ for years. He learns all music by ear. How delighted he is to discover that the new minister has first graduated as a concert pianist. Now, each Monday, a tape of the next Sunday's hymns is delivered to the undaunted Albert and his repertoire steadily increases. He is well-prepared for this Christmas Eve playing.

The church will eventually close, will become a museum, having served its community well for over twenty more years. The minister's photograph will appear on the church wall, displayed with others from before and after his own time of service.

But tonight, because of the strong faith of a few elderly women, joined by the prayerful perseverance of a dedicated group, we all share the warmth of faith and setting. Our voices rise together, gratefully acknowledging "The hopes and fears of all the years are met in thee tonight."

---

[1]Before the organ (labelled by some as "an instrument of the devil") was permitted in sanctuaries, a precentor would stand at the front of the church to lead singing or reading so that people were singing or speaking in unison. During the time that is referenced in this account, the precentor's box, which closely resembled a pulpit, was used for children's talks and for a few of the sermons.

Christmas Baby

DEIRDRE KESSLER

"AND WE WERE GOING ACROSS…"

"Who were we?

"We were all of us the same as are gathered here this evening. So, it was two days before Christmas and we were going across and it was already a hard, cold winter and…"

"Where were we going?"

"You will have to listen and be patient."

"Were we ever there before?"

"Listen and you will know. Tell me you are listening."

"I am listening. But first, could you sing a little?"

"Over the river and through the woods

To grandmother's house we go…

"We were going across all cosy in the box sleigh and the little sorrel mare was happy to be out in the sharp, fine air. The bells on the harness, you remember? How jolly it was to hear them. The runners went *shush-shush* on the hard-packed snow.

"We were going across the inlet, crossing the frozen sea water at a place your brother bushed for us. Summers we swam there and the water at low tide came only to our thighs. Another year, you went with your brother to the woods to cut young spruce, remember? Remember how you begged to go with him out on the ice to bust the track, to plant those little trees in the snow on top of the ice, a double row to guide us across?"

"Why wouldn't you let me go with him?"

"Because you were still too little and he and the mare needed to do only one thing when they set the trail. But this time, we were going across the frozen inlet, the young spruce straight and even to mark the way, the track well-tamped from our comings and goings, and this day as we were halfway across your brother said, 'Look, a sundog.'

"There it was, a spectral smear of ice crystals only a hand's breadth from the sun. Your brother clucked to the mare to hasten her trot so that we might more quickly cross to the other side. The little mare picked up her feet and the jingle and shush and snow-muffled hoofbeats made us happy. We would be across and home again before the weather turned. We were going across to get the baby, across the frozen inlet."

"Oh—this is my story! I am the baby!"

"Yes, we were going across to get the baby and bring her and the mother safe home. And the grandmother would come, too."

"I was the baby! Was I ever cute!"

"We were going across, but the mare began to flick her ears and slow her gait. Your brother clucked and slapped the reins. We were cosy in the sleigh under the buffalo robe, all woolly and warm, and in our ears the bells and shush of runners on the snow. Then the mare stopped though the way was bushed and clear, the old sleigh tracks straight and sure. The mare stopped dead and turned her head around to look at your brother.

"'Get up, Girl,' he said to her. He clucked and slapped her rump with the reins.

"She hesitated and your brother raised his voice—he raised his voice to the sorrel mare! 'HAW! GET UP!'

"She bolted forward. We heard a crack and rumble and the little mare went down. Through the ice she went, into the black sea water."

"I can't remember this part. I am too frightened to remember it."

"Yes, we were frightened, but we heard your brother's command. We jumped out of the sleigh and backed up. 'The robe!' he said. We took him the buffalo robe, close as we dared to the edge. Your brother unhitched the sleigh and pushed it back from the broken ice. And on his belly and he reached out and laid hold of the reins. He pulled the mare's head up from the black water. How low he talked to her. He turned her head around, her legs flailing, churning in the hole of broken ice.

"Remember how he grabbed the robe, slid an edge of it into the water. All the while he talked to her. Then he held the mare's chin and pulled it up onto the robe. The mare thrashed in the broken ice and mud and black water. The tide was going out. Her hind legs struck the mud beneath the ice."

"Stop! I'm too scared. I don't want to remember this story."

"'Hold my feet,' your brother commanded us. So we lay on our bellies, too, and held his boots, his calves. Your brother got hold of the mare's foreleg, talking all calm and even to her. He hauled on her and we hauled on him and the mare scrabbled her way onto the robe, up onto the ice, safe.

"You remember how your brother led her home, back to the barn. How we followed, ran to the house to make warm mash. How your brother rubbed the mare dry and fed her the good mash in the warm, safe stall."

"I remember! I was the baby on grandmother's side of the inlet, and we came home by the long road around the point, and we were in the sleigh pulled by the mare our brother rescued. And I was only new. I was the baby. I remember this story—I was the best-ever Christmas present and we were going across to fetch me home. Let's sing!"

The horse knows the way
To carry the sleigh
In the white and drifted snow-oh!

The Christmas Surprise

DEBORAH GRAHAM

I CAN ONLY IMAGINE what it must have been like for those visitors who dropped by to see my grandparents' tree during the Christmas season of 1934. On December 13, my grandfather rushed across town to fetch the local doctor. "Hurry, Dr. Stuart!" he said breathlessly. "My wife's gone into labour and she's about to deliver our baby."

It wasn't an easy birth but a few minutes before 6 P.M., the baby made her way into the world. Dr. Stuart knew the baby would be small as my grandmother, Flora, only gained five pounds throughout her entire pregnancy. Even so he became alarmed at how tiny she truly was. She fit into the palm of his hand. In order for the scales to register the baby's weight, the doctor added a bar of "Surprise" soap to his scales to bring her weight up to a full pound.

The baby was too delicate to nurse, so Flora carefully fed her with an eye dropper. Typical newborn clothing was useless, so Grammy wrapped her baby in pieces of soft cloth. The family kept her warm in a homemade incubator made from a cardboard shoebox lined with pieces of soft cloth warmed by the wood stove. The baby thrived in her small world, but even after a year she was only able to wear clothing made for a twelve-inch doll.

I've been told it is a miracle such a small baby survived back then. Even today with our modern technology, underweight babies are at risk and have to be cared for in hospitals until they reach a near-normal birth weight. The miracle of this birth didn't go unnoticed. News quickly spread throughout the town, and the baby became the centre of attention as family and friends gathered around to "ooh" and "ahh."

Yes, I can only imagine what it must have been like for those visitors who dropped by that Christmas and found the baby wrapped in swaddling clothes and lying in a shoebox.

One would hardly expect a humble shoebox to hold such a precious surprise—my mother, Doreen.

Sarah's Gifts

LESLEY CREWE

I WAS SO DESPERATELY UNHAPPY the Christmas of 1985. Our little boy Joshua had died only the month before, and the thought of our four-year-old son Paul without his little brother on Christmas morning was more than I could bear.

I don't remember much about that Christmas Day except that the house was full of relatives and I was grateful. It was as if they knew I couldn't cope, so they trooped in and made lots of noise and excitement for Paul, and cooked a turkey with all the trimmings. I spent most of the day smiling whenever Paul came near me, and staying quiet when he left the room. I had no energy for anyone or anything.

I went to the cemetery and sat in the snow. Everyone knew where I was going and left me alone. When I got back, I went in the nursery and rocked in the rocking chair, hugging one of Joshua's favourite bears. I didn't go near his closet because I knew that's where his Christmas presents were, the ones I bought for him only a few hours before he suddenly stopped breathing.

John spent the day in the basement. He pretended to tinker with something or other and drank beer. I do remember going downstairs to tell him dinner was ready and he looked at me with big sad eyes.

"Do I have to?" he said. I just nodded.

Somehow we lived through that miserable, awful winter and one spring day I went to the doctor to confirm what I already knew in my heart. A new baby was coming. The doctor smiled at me. "You're going to have a Christmas baby. You're due December 25th."

I was scared to death. I'd like to say I was thrilled, but I was mostly terrified, with just brief moments of happiness peeking around the corner. I was almost afraid to love this baby, in case something happened. My broken heart was still broken and I was fragile.

But I'll never forget the day I told Paul. I sat him on my lap and said, "Mommy's going to have a Christmas baby." He didn't say anything at first. He got off my lap and went in the other room. I knew he was frightened too, so I left him alone. But about five minutes later he came back and hugged my leg. "I really like you, Mommy."

Of course the closer I got to December 25th, the more worried I became. I wanted to be home with Paul on Christmas Day. Surely this little monkey would wait a few more days. I'd been late with both of the boys, so I assumed the same thing would happen, but it wasn't to be. On December 22nd, my contractions started and I had to kiss Paul goodbye, knowing I wouldn't be home for Christmas.

I was so nervous. I knew the baby was safe inside me. I didn't want it to come out and take that first breath, because maybe it would stop breathing. The doctor assured me he'd never had a mother yet who could keep her legs crossed for too long!

And he was right. At five minutes before midnight on the 22nd our daughter Sarah was born. She let out one almighty scream and that should have assured me right then and there she was a force to be reckoned with and had no intention of going anywhere. Then her bottom lip came out and she pouted at her father, and to this day, that's all she has to do and he's putty in her hands.

That Christmas morning, as I nursed Sarah in my hospital room, the phone rang. It was Paul. "Guess what I just got for Christmas," he shouted. "A new truck!" I never got a chance to say, "Wow," before he yelled, "Just a minute,

Mommy, I'll be right back," and he tore off. I heard him opening another gift with a shout of glee, and he was soon back on the phone again. "Guess what? I got a He-Man!"

"You're kidding," I laughed, but he wasn't there to hear it. He was gone again.

This was our Christmas morning. John and Paul arrived at the hospital later that day so Paul could show Sarah his gifts. What he didn't know was that his dad had only put half of them under the tree, saving the other half for when Sarah and I could be there. Finally on December 27th, Sarah and I went home. Paul took great delight in showing her the Christmas tree and was thrilled to find more gifts under it. He also took great pleasure in giving Sarah her gifts.

"I wonder what Santa got for Sarah?"

I knew what was inside those presents. Joshua's gifts were finally being opened by his little sister, which his big brother's help.

"Two Christmases! Are we ever lucky, Sarah!"

John and I looked at each other. At that moment, the five of us were together.

My Christmas Miracle

ANNE CORMIER

CHRISTMAS HAS ALWAYS BEEN AN EXCITING TIME, a blessed time for me.

For years, my most memorable Christmas was that of 1968. It was to be my mother's last celebration with me and my dad. She died in May of 1969, when I was just ten years old. But nothing can ever compare to the extraordinary Christmas of 1990 when my husband and I celebrated a Christmas so unique that nothing will ever outshine the memory.

When Danny and I married in 1981, we knew we wanted children. My husband is one of nine, and I was an only child. For both of us, family was important. During the early years, we were unconcerned about the fact that I did not become pregnant. After all, we were still young. However, in 1986, when I began to develop tumours and faced surgery, we then were forced to acknowledge that something was indeed wrong.

After trips to several doctors, I was finally sent to a fertility clinic in Halifax. Here, several doctors examined me and came to the shocking conclusion that I would never have a child due to a rare condition. "I'm sorry; there is just nothing we can do. For you to have a child would be a miracle," one endocrinologist firmly told me. Danny and I were devastated. In the doctor's words, there was no hope at all.

Over the next few weeks and months, I tried to dismiss it from my mind. They could be wrong after all, I reasoned. And we were still young; there was still time. Maybe a new medical advance would change things.

Then in January of 1989, the unbelievable happened. I discovered I was pregnant! My family doctor could not believe the results. He sent me for an Ultrasound and more blood work. When my doctor called me at home early on a Sunday morning to discuss the findings with me he was almost as excited as we were. "This is what we always prayed for and it is probably your only chance."

I was so excited I couldn't think clearly. When I tried to drive I couldn't focus because I was too excited and solidly stuck in a snow bank.

Unfortunately, my excitement came to an abrupt end, when on March 21, I miscarried at five months.

If the 1987 report from the fertility specialists was devastating, it was nothing compared to this. I cried for weeks. How could this happen?

Since I had been off work since January, I extended my time and stayed off until May, at the suggestion of my doctor. I couldn't focus on work anyway, and had trouble dealing with the day-to-day tasks.

During this time, Danny and I both had a dream, and were given hope that we would have another child. In January of 1990, our dreams and hopes became a reality. I was pregnant again! On November 6, 1990, I had a nine pound, nine-and-a-half ounce boy, who we named Marc Daniel.

Christmas took on a whole new focus. I couldn't wait to decorate. I wrote out my Christmas cards with the baby sleeping on my lap or sometimes cuddled up to me in a "Snugly."

Over the next few weeks, I took him to each choir practice and smiled as he was lovingly passed around and cuddled by my friends. My friend who had a little girl four weeks before did the same. We sang as we held our babies and then when our arms were tired, we passed them on to someone nearby. That Christmas the whole choir juggled babies and music books and smiled while doing so. It was an unbelievably special time. I had never enjoyed choir practice so much.

When Christmas Eve finally arrived, all was in order. The house was decorated; the turkey was ready for the oven. In the early evening Danny's sister and her husband arrived with their five-month-old son. They would be spending the holiday with us. As I looked around that room, my happiness knew no bounds. Two couples with two precious little baby boys.

Danny and I didn't give gifts to each other that year; we were blessed with what we had. We had a gift that no money could buy, a little gem with big brown eyes and a crop of dark hair.

On Christmas Day, as we celebrated the birth of the Christ child born in a stable long ago, the day took on even greater meaning for me as I held my new son. I put him in his small chair and sat him under the tree. His eyes glowed as he gazed at the twinkling lights above him. And I took a photo that will forever be a treasure to me.

As we look at that photo now and recall the moment, we share with Marc the love and the happiness he brought into our lives. As I look at the picture of that small baby in his little red overalls underneath a Christmas tree, I'm reminded that life is precious and that the greatest gifts are not in what we buy, they are found in those we love.

We received an incomparable gift that year, a gift from God, a miracle, our son, Marc.

A Christmas to Remember

EVELYN NOLAN

MANY YEARS AGO, I ended up breaking my leg fairly close to Christmas. Going down the stairs at home, the heel of my shoe got caught in the carpet on the stairs. I fell and my foot stayed in the shoe and the shoe in the carpet. Needless to say I ended up with a broken ankle. My father had died and we were getting ready to go to his funeral.

I had worked many years and never collected unemployment so in filling out my forms I made a mistake and the forms were sent back. In talking to my fellow staff members I expressed my disappointment and said to them, "What am I going to do for Christmas?" Having three children was going to make Christmas hard.

That next week was pay week and I still would not have had enough money for even the

Christmas necessities. To my surprise, the day after pay day my staff presented me with a large box of groceries which left me money to buy a few gifts for the boys and pay some bills. The boys also put our name in the Empty Stocking Fund without telling me (as I was too proud to ask.).

Thank God for my boys and my staff as that year we truly had a blessed Christmas. I would like to say thank you and God bless them all.

Of Waiting Rooms and Russian Blues

JENNIFER KENT

DESPITE THE TINNY CAROLS warbling from the loudspeaker mounted above the door of the corner convenience store, I was feeling less-than-Christmasy as I slopped along the slushy sidewalk, my two preschoolers firmly in tow. Sure, the holiday brought with it the decorations, the angel lights along Main Street, the Christmas pageants at the local churches, the neighbourhood cookie exchanges…but the flip side to Christmas in New Brunswick is that it coincides almost exactly with flu season.

And so I found myself making yet another pilgrimage to the doctor's office. I sighed, hitched up the diaper bag that kept slipping off my shoulder, scooped one wayward son down from his foray up a soggy snow bank, and wearily climbed the steps of the seventy-five-year-old house that is our doctor's office.

I glanced around the tiny room full of snuffling, sneezing people crowded into chairs around the coffee table with its avalanche of *Reader's Digests* and old *Field & Stream* magazines. Yup, an hour and a half minimum, I thought to myself. I peeled the kids out of their snowsuits and shoved the diaper bag under the steel-framed chair with its fraying, mustard-yellow upholstery. The boys launched themselves at the battered laundry basket full of equally battered toys.

I eased myself gingerly into my chair, wedged shoulder-to-shoulder between a mother holding a child with copious amounts of fluid flowing freely from her nose, and an older gentleman who hawked loudly into a discoloured handkerchief at surprisingly regular intervals. I tried to breathe as shallowly as possible.

The afternoon dragged on. We waited in silence, wearied by the journey that had brought each of us here, feigning polite obliviousness towards each other's existence. There was no room. No room in this crowded place to admit that we were all swaddled in the same tattered clothes of the human condition. No room to acknowledge each other's frailties. The radio, tuned to CBC, began to play "Hark the Herald Angels Sing." Somewhere, in a backroom, a newborn baby began to cry.

By now it was late in the day and the early winter darkness was already clawing at the windows. I was mentally checking off the presents that still needed to be purchased and wrapped, the cards that still needed to be sent, and the sweets that still needed to be baked, when the door jingled open one more time. The waiting room, at long last, had almost emptied when an older man lumbered in. He was wearing a red and black plaid flannel woodsman's coat and a stained T-shirt stretched to capacity over his bulging belly. A few straggly locks of lank, grey hair curled well below his ears. The rest was hidden beneath a greasy ball cap that read "Mosquito Cove Fire Department." The pungent aroma of grease, oil, wood-smoke and hard labour followed him into the room. People moved their magazines a little closer to their noses. The man kicked off a gigantic pair of mud-encrusted rubber boots, poled his newly-liberated toes, and sank heavily into a chair with a loud sigh and a groan. I couldn't help noticing his two remaining top teeth moved in and out as he breathed—like curtains in a breeze.

Unlike most of the other waiting room occupants, this man did not pick up a magazine, nor did he retreat behind that vacant, glassy-eyed stare we so often employ in crowded places. Instead, he regarded the room around him with an animated eye. He listened attentively as I read quietly to my sons and he exclaimed in disappointment when the chapter ended and I closed the book. He chuckled at the antics of my boys and they, sensing his genuine interest, happily showed him the mangled treasures they had rummaged from the bottom of the toy basket.

My children were oblivious to this man's appearance and aroma. They saw only an adult who was genuinely interested in what they had to say. As they scurried back to the toys, the man shook his head indulgently and remarked to the room at large, "They sure are lively…just like my kittens!"

"You keep cats?" I ventured, politely.

"Four kittens and their mother!" he declared. His chest swelled with pride. "The mother's a Russian blue. She came to me one night, lost, in the middle of a snowstorm. And pregnant! She had nowhere to go so I took her in and cared for her." He shook his head. "A beautiful animal like that should never have been left outside!"

For the next twenty minutes he spoke with gentle affection about his cats. He told me how when he leaves his feline family to go to work for the day, he puts out three clean bowls of water…and how they will have drunk exactly one and a half by the time he gets home. I listened, fascinated, as the gnarly, old woodsman talked about the best places to buy pet food and cat toys, and confided to me which brand of canned sardines was best for conditioning the coat. I asked him if he was going to keep the kittens. His brow furrowed.

"They are such a close-knit little family. I sure would hate to break them up!" He then launched into a long account of his cats' various escapades. His eyes shone as he spoke. It was clear the kittens were home to stay.

I was almost sorry when the nurse at last motioned us to the exam room.

Later that night, after my children had fallen asleep listening to Christmas carols, I went to the computer and looked up "Russian blue." These cats, said the web site, were the preferred pets of kings and queens, aristocratic animals descended of royalty.

I thought about the royal cat who had sought shelter in the humblest of homes. I thought about nobility cloaked in human frailty, and how the divine may be revealed in the most unexpected of places, at the most unexpected of times. Where else but in a waiting room would I have had the opportunity to discover this man's joy and to discuss at length his love for a Russian blue?

I scrolled a little further down the web page. And there it was: according to legend, the Russian blue was originally known as the archangel cat.

The archangel cat.

I turned off the computer and sat looking out the window. Choirs sang, the heavens wheeled, and there in the night sky, a great star winked at me, looking for all the world like a cat's eye. And I understood that joy treads on silent paws out of the darkest night, bringing richness to the poorest parts of our lives. All we have to do is notice it…and let it inside.

The Re-Gift Specials

CINDY ETTER-TURNBULL

ONE FALL, my mother had given us some preserves, many more than we would ever use. Among them were stewed plums from our own trees. Since no one in our household liked stewed plums, I decided to give them to my brother-in-law for Christmas.

The next Christmas, much to my surprise, he gave them back to me. We have kept passing this same bottle of plums for more than ten years.

The bottle is covered with Christmas tags and travels in the same bag it was first delivered in. Of course, the trick now is to try and smuggle it under the tree without being seen. It has become a fun family tradition.

I do, however, pity the poor soul who tries to open and eat these rather rusty looking blobs of mush.

Along the same lines, my cousin Linda and I have been passing back and forth a treasured box on Christmas Eve. This grey cardboard box measures six by ten inches (yes, inches—it was born in the inches era), and has a colourful image of a Victorian Santa on the cover. The sides of the box are red, the corners are starting to come apart and nicks and tears are apparent along its edges. It has the smell of old cardboard and its overall structure is sagging.

I can't remember which of us gave it to the other first, but we have been trading this wonderful little item for more than thirty years! Most people would have tossed a tattered old box like this away years ago. To Linda and me, this box is very special. It isn't the gift in the box that matters so much, it is the rich tradition and loving bond the box symbolizes.

Kindness—
the Christmas Gift That Lasts

ELAINE INGALLS HOGG

I WAS SEVEN YEARS OLD when I learned the meaning of kindness. It was a lesson I was to remember for the rest of my life. On December 24th, pale and frail after a two-month stay in hospital, I arrived home in my aunt's car. As soon as I was in the house, the family greeted me with plenty of hugs and kisses. Their prayers had been answered, the family would be together for Christmas and everyone was happy.

"Come, come see," my brother Norman tugged me by the hand and pulled me into the living room. "Look at the tree. It has real lights, not candles. Mom, will you put the lights on for us?"

I stood motionless in front of the tree and watched as my mother turned on the lights. "Oh! It's so pretty!" my voice was barely a whisper as I admired the coloured lights and the delicate glass balls.

"Look, look, Sis!" five-year-old Norman was excited. He had actually missed me and he wanted to show me everything at once. "There's a present here for all of us!" He crawled under the tree and pointed out the names on the brightly wrapped packages. See! This one's your present. It says Elaine Marie on it."

"That's nice but tomorrow morning I'm going to have more presents than anybody in the whole wide world."

"No you're not!"

"Yes I am! The nurses thought I was going to stay in the hospital for Christmas and they bought me lots of presents. They're in that box over there." Gleefully I pointed to a large cardboard box near the suitcase I had brought from the hospital. "It's full of presents and I can hardly wait to open them all." At that precise moment my parents exchanged worried looks. Later I heard them talking through the curtain that divided their sleeping area from ours in the upstairs bedroom. "How can we allow Elaine to have more presents than her brothers? I know she's been away for a long time, but the boys won't understand when they see her open all those gifts."

"I know, I've been thinking about that ever since she came home," my mother's voice was soft and thoughtful. "After the boys are to sleep, I think I'll have a talk with her. She's seven now, perhaps she's old enough to go along with my plan."

At bedtime my mother sat at the edge of my bed and talked to me. When she was finished she hugged me and left the room hoping that everything would work out.

On Christmas morning I was the first one downstairs. I reached for the big box and pulled it out from under the tree. My two younger brothers, Norman and Laurie, watched me untie the ribbon and pick at the tape trying not to tear the paper. "Hurry Sis! You're too slow," they urged. Finally the box was open and when they saw the coloured packages they asked, "Are all those presents really just for you?"

"Well I guess this present's mine. A boy wouldn't want a pink pyjama doll!"

"Is all that there is—girl's stuff?" Norman sounded disappointed.

"No, here's something a boy can play with. You can have these." And I passed him a book and some building blocks. "And Laurie, here's something for you." My baby brother toddled over and took the cuddly teddy bear in his arms. When I was finished dividing up the presents in the box, I said, "Look Mom, I shared and I still have the most presents."

"I see," she said and once again her voice had a thoughtful

tone. I could tell she had more to say. "I was thinking, two dolls might be one too many when I know a little girl who won't have any presents this year. Pick which one you'd like to give her and we'll take it to her after breakfast."

"That's not what I had in mind," my bottom lip stuck out in a full-sized pout. "Mom, I already shared!" But there was no arguing with Mom. She had made up her mind and I soon figured if I didn't pick soon, my mother would pick for me. I'd never had many toys and now I'd fallen in love with both dolls but after a few moments I decided to keep the Eaton's Beauty Doll. I had been watching her in the catalogue for months and I already had a name for her: Rilla Jean, Glenna Juanita, Linda Pandora, I would name her after all my favourite people in the whole world.

I hugged the pink pyjama doll one more time, kissed her on the cheek then helped my mother wrap her in a box to take to some other child. "I hope she likes you," I whispered with tears in my eyes. Giving away something you loved so much is hard, I decided.

Later that morning Mother and daughter made deep footsteps in the swirling snow. We didn't stop at the small neat house at the end of the lane but instead we continued to a fisherman's shed down near the shore. The door opened to the workshop and smelled of wood shavings. "Who's there?" a muffled voice called down the ladder from a hatch door in the ceiling. "George, it's Audrey and Elaine Marie. We brought Penny a present."

"Come on up," he invited but as soon as we went through the hatch door he was apologizing for their situation. "I'd ask to take your coats but it's a bit cold here still. We were all in bed so I didn't put the stove on."

I looked all around the tiny attic room with its sloped ceilings and small window on the gable end. The black and white stove with an oven door hanging by one hinge took up most of one end of the room and next to it was a couple of covered orange crates used to store a few dishes. The bed was in the middle of the room because the painted brass headboard didn't fit under the eaves. It surprised me to find my friend Penny and her mother still in bed. There was no knit stocking with an orange in the toe like I had found in mine this morning; in fact there were no signs of Christmas anywhere.

I walked to Penny's side of the bed. "Here, I brought you a present. I hope you like it," and I thrust the package with the smoothed out wrapping paper and retied ribbon into the little girl's arms.

Later when we got ready to leave Mr. Black kept rubbing his hands through his hair. "Audrey, Elaine, how did you know?" I thought the big man was going to cry. "Your kindness will always be remembered," he said as mother and I made our way back down the ladder.

Contributors

Laura Best lives in East Dalhousie, Nova Scotia, along with her husband and son. For about eight months of the year she works in the Christmas tree industry, leaving her several months in the winter to write to her heart's content. Most recently, her short fiction has been accepted for publication in *Grain*, *Transition* and *The Dalhousie Review*.

David Betts was born in Amherst, and attended Dalhousie University. He was a reporter and editor for seven years with the *Halifax Chronicle-Herald*, then an editor with the Canadian Press in Toronto before moving to England in the 1960s. He worked for Reuters, the international news organization, for thirty-seven years as an editor, correspondent, broadcaster, manager and, finally, trainer of young journalists. He and his wife Trixie live in Dorset, England, but spend three summer months each year at their family home in Wallace, Nova Scotia.

Sandra Boutquin currently lives in Toronto where she works for a major music company. However, her roots are on the east coast and she visits her brother and daughter there whenever she can. She has a son, three daughters, and three grandchildren. She is a piper with Hamilton Police Pipe Band and enjoys writing. She previously contributed an article to *When Canada Meets Cape Breton*, a book commemorating the fiftieth anniversary of the opening of the Canso Causeway.

Jamie Bradley is a west-end Halifax boy and, having grown up in the shadows of three shopping malls, knows his Santas. He has written a multitude of dinner theatres, plays, puppet plays, and musical revues for the Harbourfront Jubilee Theatre in Summerside, PEI and Roy Thompson Hall in Toronto. CBC radio has presented Jamie's radio dramas, monologues, and commentaries, and he is a former movie reviewer for CBC television. Jamie's wife and kids are extremely patient people.

Donna Buckley was born and raised in Saint John and graduated from Mount Carmel Academy in 1958. She later attended Northern Essex Community College in Massachusetts and Beal College in Maine. After living in the United States for thirty-five years, she recently returned to the Saint John area. She has been writing stories of family happenings for many years, and the selection included here has always been a favourite.

Anne-Marie Caissie is a member of the Writers' Federation of New Brunswick and Professional Writers Association of Canada, and her many interests enable her to write on a variety of topics. Anne-Marie writes book reviews for the *Daily Gleaner* newspaper, volunteers for Habitat for Humanity Fredericton Area, and is a regular contributor in their quarterly newsletter. She enjoys writing for children and is working on a collection of short stories. She lives in Fredericton.

Harry Chapman is a long-time resident of Dartmouth. He worked at the *Halifax Herald* as a news reporter/photographer at the Dartmouth news bureau, where he was later appointed editor and bureau chief. He joined the Nova Scotia government as a communications officer in 1980 and retired in 1997. He has written eight books on topics of local interest. His history of Dartmouth, *In the Wake of the Alderney*, won the Dartmouth Writing Award in 2001.

Anne Burke Cormier grew up in St. Peters, Richmond County. She graduated from Nova Scotia Teacher's College in 1980 and attended St. Francis Xavier University. She worked with special needs students for many years and currently resides in Port Hawkesbury with her husband Daniel, son Marc, and her beagle companion, "Shadow." She enjoys reading, writing, gardening, walking her dog, playing music with a church worship band, and photography.

Montreal-born Lesley Crewe earned a B.A. in English from Concordia University before moving to Homeville, Cape Breton, to raise her family. She was a columnist and features writer for *The Cape Bretoner* magazine. She now writes a column ("Lesley's Letters") for the new women's magazine, *Cahoots*. She published her first novel, *Relative Happiness*, in September 2005 (short-listed for the Margaret and John Savage First Book Award). Her second novel, *Shoot Me*, will be published in September 2006.

Clary Croft lives in Halifax and is a folklore researcher and folk singer. The author of *Chocolates, Tattoos and Mayflowers* and *Helen Creighton: Canada's First Lady of Folklore*, his book *Celebrate! The History and Folklore of Holidays* in Nova Scotia is now part of the Nova Scotia school curriculum. Clary's most recent Nimbus publication, *Nova Scotia Moments*, is a collection of history and folklore items from his daily broadcasts on the Maritimes's Information Radio stations.

Roger Cyr was born in Cumberland County, Nova Scotia, and for his first eleven years lived with his grandmother in New Prospect. During a twenty-five-year career with the RCAF he served on three continents. His writing has appeared in *Shadows of War, Faces of Peace: Canada's Peacekeepers* and *When Canada Joined Cape Breton*. Now retired, he lives in the Annapolis Valley, Nova Scotia.

Born and educated in England, **Joan Dawson** has lived in Halifax since 1960. Married to the late English professor and printer, Bob Dawson, she has been a mother, teacher, librarian, researcher, writer, translator, and grandmother. She is a member of Heritage Trust of Nova Scotia and a Fellow of the Royal Nova Scotia Historical Society. When not busy with any of these activities, she enjoys reading, traveling and gardening.

Professor **David Divine** is the James Robinson Johnston Chair in Black Canadian Studies at Dalhousie University (jamesrjohnstonchair.dal.ca). He has a background in working with the most powerless in the community and jointly working with such individuals and communities to find ways of redressing injustices. Professor Divine came to Canada in January 2004, and his wife, Ann, and three children, David, Davinia, and Ephraim, joined him eight months later. They reside in Halifax.

Kelly Douglas is a native of Ontario and has lived in Fredericton several times with her husband, a military officer, and her son. She enjoys making various crafts, baking, antiques, and reading. Christmas is her favourite time of the year for many reasons. The story that appears in this collection is one of her best memories of her grandfather, who passed away in 1990.

Ruth Beairsto Edgett grew up on the north shore of Prince Edward Island, daughter of a born-and-bred Islander father and a mother from "the other side" (Nova Scotia). Ruth wrote for a living for more than twenty years and now writes for pleasure. She is just completing a book, to be published by Nimbus in 2007, based on the experiences of her mother's lightkeeping family. She lives in Ancaster, Ontario, with her husband Scott.

Devonna Edwards was born in Halifax, the eldest daughter of John and Mary O'Brien's ten children. She worked as a nurse for twenty-five years and at present lives in Lower Sackville with her husband of thirty-seven years, Donnie. She has two grown sons, Donald and Darcy, and a grandson, Dylan. She is the author of two books, *Wartime Recipes From The Maritimes* and *The Little Dutch Village*. She spends her free time researching and writing local history.

Patricia Anne Elford, a Canadian writer published in various genres and a professional member of The Word Guild, is also an editor, educator, motivational speaker, Presbyterian minister, and, periodically, a civilian officiating chaplain at the CFB Petawawa Protestant chapel. She is also a wife, mother of five and a grandmother. Patricia and her husband are entertained, and dictated to, by Bagheera and Lickorish, two long-tailed ebony cats, in "The Pines," their home in Ontario's Ottawa Valley.

After a twenty-year career working with mentally challenged adults, first-time author **Cindy Etter-Turnbull** followed her writing instincts and fascination with rural culture. Her love of tradition, beauty, and humour led to her book *Fine Lines* and to establishing a website, mrs-clothesline.com. When the mother of Nathan and Jon is not hanging out laundry, she is gardening or fishing with her husband, Chris. Their comfy family home rests in Avondale, Nova Scotia.

Christina Flemming graduated in 2006 with a Bachelor of Journalism degree with honours from the University of King's College. After traveling throughout Spain, Greece, the Czech Republic, and France, her love for Nova Scotia remains strong. Currently, she lives in Halifax and hopes one day to have her own home with a ceiling high enough to continue the family tradition of choosing Titanic-sized Christmas trees.

Sean Flinn lives in Halifax, where he works as a freelance journalist, with his wife Sue and cat Lucy. He writes short fiction and is working on a novel based on his grandparents, Jakob and Laine Suksdorf, who fled Estonia for Sweden in 1944 and then moved to Canada, landing in Halifax in 1949.

Joyce Gero has been crafting stories for family and friends since she was a child. An administrative assistant for a manufacturing company in Truro, Nova Scotia, Joyce has served on the staff of her company's quarterly newsmagazine, and has been published in a trade journal and a small chapbook from Craigleigh Press. A grandmother of four, she shares an apartment with two fat cats and a growing collection of books, manuscripts, and unfinished craft projects.

Gillian has been writing professionally since her mid-twenties when she received fifty dollars to script some comedic sketches for the year-end show of Hamilton Theatresports. In addition to young adult novels (*Willow Heights* will be

published by Nimbus in 2007) and adult fiction, she also
writes plays with her partner, Frank McEnaney. They live in
Wolfville, Nova Scotia, with their seven-year-old daughter,
Risa.

Joleen Gordon grew up in Halifax and now makes her
home near Lake Banook in Dartmouth. For the past thirty
years, she has been a research associate with the Nova Scotia Museum recording the many basket-making traditions
of the founding people of Nova Scotia.

David Goss lives in Saint John and operates a popular walking program where he shares stories and historical tidbits. He has written a column on local lore for the
New Brunswick Telegraph Journal since 1989. In addition, his
stories have appeared in various Canadian and American
newspapers, major Maritime magazines, and several national magazines. He has also authored ten books of local
stories for three different publishers. Of all the tales he
tells, he says those about his family, and especially those
about his family at Christmas, are his favourites.

Deborah Graham lives in Sussex, New Brunswick with
her husband Ivan. They have been married for thirty-one
years and have two grown children. Deborah is a graduate
of Bethany Bible College where she now volunteers in
the donor development and planned giving department.
She is an active member of her church, where she mentors
women, hosts a mid-week Bible study and teaches others
how to achieve their personal financial goals. In her spare
time, she enjoys writing, gardening and decorating.

Monica Graham wrote "Don't Worry. We'll Have Christmas Tomorrow" as one of a series of yet-to-be-published
short stories in tongue-in-cheek tribute to husbands. The
Pictou County, Nova Scotia, freelance journalist and col-

umnist is published regularly in Halifax's *The Chronicle Herald*, and has written three books. She is currently working on a biography for Nimbus Publishing.

Mildred A. Gregory resides in Rothesay, New Brunswick with her husband, Sandy. After an enjoyable career ranging from senior administrative positions to the federal civil service, she is now retired and travel, golf, and visiting family members across Canada keep her busy. She finds recalling Christmas memories most gratifying.

Elaine Ingalls Hogg is an inspirational speaker and the author of *When Canada Joined Cape Breton* and *Remembering Honey*. An avid storyteller, Elaine has told stories to children from Nova Scotia to New Zealand. Her writing has been included in anthologies such as the Chicken Soup series, *God Allows U-Turns* and *Soul Matters for Moms*. Elaine, her husband Hugh, and their mischievous, geriatric pet, Ben Nevis, now live near Sussex, New Brunswick.

David G. Jones is the son of the late Evelyn Collins and stepson of Jimmy Collins of Glace Bay. He is a management consultant, author and lecturer who resides in Ottawa with his Annapolis Valley wife, Ena Gwen. They have three children, Jeela, Martin and Evan. The Joneses spend as much of their time as they can at their cottage in Trout Lake, Annapolis County.

Jennifer McGrath Kent is a children's storyteller, essayist, playwright, and freelance writer. Her multifarious interests are reflected in her eclectic choice of writing topics, which range from Celtic spirituality to alpacas. Jennifer lives just outside Moncton with her husband, two young sons, a dog, a cat, and a Welsh Cob pony.

Deirdre Kessler is a Charlottetown-based author of ten books for young people, including the Canadian Children's Book Centre Our Choice Award-winning *Brupp Rides Again* and *Lobster in My Pocket*. A chapbook of her poems, *Subtracting by Seventeen*, was published in 2005 and a new children's book, *Dreamtime*, illustrated by Cecily Donnelly, will be published in autumn 2006. She teaches creative writing and children's literature in the English department at the University of Prince Edward Island.

Darlene Lawson is an inspirational writer/storyteller. She and her husband live on a farm in Kent County, New Brunswick. Darlene has been published in various magazines, four *Chicken Soup for the Soul* books, and an anthology of Canadian stories. She works as a freelance reporter for a community paper. Darlene credits her writing abilities to being in touch with the beauty of God's handiwork that surrounds their farm.

Christine Lovelace, an ordinary Maritimer, would love to return to the Maritimes forever someday, but for now works as an archivist in Washington, D. C. Her memories of growing up in New Brunswick and living in Halifax for the past ten years are the only things that keep her sane while in exile. This is her very first published work and she is tickled pink.

A very senior citizen, Loretta Jean Mackinnon was born, raised, married, and widowed in Sydney Mines, Cape Breton. Around age seventy she began to write stories of her childhood. She has had a story published in *The Cape Bretoner* and a few of her stories have also been read on CBC Radio. She has also read and related some of her stories at a monthly storytelling session in her hometown. She believes that memories are precious and will continue to enjoy writing about them.

Blake Maybank, born in Alberta and raised in Saskatchewan, is a "born-again Bluenoser," a resident of White's Lake since 1987. He's addicted to Nova Scotia's nature, and is the author of *Birding Sites of Nova Scotia* and *National Parks and Other Wild Places of Canada*. Blake is also a public speaker, photographer, musician, and organizer of nature tours worldwide. His wife is Martine Dufresene, a professional translator and amateur botanist from Quebec.

Evelyn Nolan was born near Bathurst but moved to Saint John when she was very young. Except for one year in Montreal, she has lived in the city all her life, growing up in the city road area. As a young girl she loved swimming and spending time at the park with her mother. She likes writing poetry and has her own Geocities website.

Bruce Nunn is a journalist, storyteller, broadcaster, writer, and professional communicator based in Halifax. Also known by the tongue-in-cheek title "Mr. Nova Scotia Know-It-All," he has researched and presented hundreds of uniquely Nova Scotian history stories on CBC radio and CBC television, in newspapers, magazines, keynote talks, and three books: *History with a Twist*, *More History with a Twist*, and *59 Stories*. His children's books include: *The Magical Christmas Light of Old Nova Scotia* and *Buddy the Bluenose Reindeer*. In 2006, his storytelling earned him a Gold Award from the Atlantic Journalism Association.

John Payzant was born in Halifax in 1944. After schooling in Halifax and Dartmouth, he attended Queen's University where he graduated in 1968 with an honours degree in Commerce. Thereafter, he moved to Toronto where he spent the following thirty-six years working on Bay Street in the financial services industry. He and his wife, Carolyn Hogg, retired to Lunenburg in 2004. Payzant now builds furniture and writes stories.

The late **Clarice Poirier** (née Doucet) grew up in the small Prince Edward Island community of Palmer Road. Married in 1927 to Edmund Poirier, she moved with her family to the Toronto area in the mid-1950s, and later, to Victoria, British Columbia. Clarice has eight children and many more grandchildren. She died in 1999, two years to the day after she and her husband celebrated their seventieth wedding anniversary. This is her only known published work.

Beth Powning and her artist husband, Peter Powning, moved to a farm near Sussex, New Brunswick, in 1972, where they still live. Their son, Jake, is a sword maker. Beth Powning has contributed articles and photographs to many books, magazines, and anthologies. Her own books include *Seeds of Another Summer*, *Shadow Child*, *The Hatbox Letters*, and *Edge Seasons*. She is currently at work on a new novel.

Despite having published ten nonfiction books, **Gary Ic. Saunders** still feels most at home with the informal essay and its city cousin, the magazine piece. Since 1961, counting east coast magazines and venues like *Canadian Geographic*, *Reader's Digest*, *Canadian Living*, *Nature Canada* (as a columnist) and *American Forests*, he's published over two hundred. He says he picked the dog story mostly because he still misses Sidney, especially at Christmas.

Born in Hamilton, Ontario, **Harvey Sawler's** travels as a tourism industry consultant have exposed him to countless people and situations ideal for creating stories. He writes for *Saltscapes* and *Progress* magazines and has written five books including the novels *The Penguin Man*, *One Single Hour*, and *Saving Mrs. Kennedy*. His non-fiction works include *The Beer Bandit Caper* and *On The Road With Dutch Mason* (co-author). He is currently working on several books, including a detailed examination of the Irving family and their enterprises, forthcoming from Nimbus in 2007.

Tom Sheppard lives near Kejimkujik National Park, where he and his wife, Sheila, have raised two children. He was principal of the North Queens Schools and is a long-time columnist with the *Liverpool Advance*. He has a degree in political science from Acadia and graduate degrees in international studies from Carleton and educational administration from the University of Toronto. He is the author of *Historic Queens County*, *Historic Wolfville*, and co-author of *Keji: A Guide*.

Audrey Straight began writing seriously in 2001 when she began submitting material to the "Memories" section of the New Brunswick *Telegraph-Journal*. She has written a history of the first Saint John Girl Guide Company, where she was a leader for many years. She is delighted to see her Christmas memories of Toyland in print. She lives in Saint John.

Alan Syliboy is a Mi'kmaq artist who studied at the Nova Scotia College of Art and Design. His paintings and original prints combine traditional petroglyph symbols with contemporary designs. Alan has his own fine arts studio and company, Red Crane Enterprises, that not only sells his own work, but that of other native artists, including carvers, painters, and traditional craft makers. He lives on the Millbrook First Nation reserve in Truro.

Charles Thompson is a retired area chief of conservation for the Department of Fisheries and Oceans. He has contributed regular op-ed pieces for Victoria County's bimonthly *Victoria Standard*, and since 1998, he has also written a column for the *Cape Breton Post* called "View from the Highlands." He has also published a story in the *Atlantic Salmon Journal*, the voice of salmon fishermen world wide. He is married to Ann, and has one daughter, Emily.

Since joining the Chronicle-Herald in 1984, Len Wagg has covered numerous assignments in Nova Scotia, across Canada and the United States, and overseas. His photographs have appeared in the *New York Times*, *Time*, *Maclean's* and other newspapers around the world. Len is the author of *Nova Scotia Landmarks: Portrait of a Province from the Air* (2004) and the editor of *Chronicle of Our Time* (2005).

Budge Wilson was born and raised in Nova Scotia, and now lives in a fishing village on the south shore. She has published thirty-two books for both children and adults, with editions in nine other languages. Budge has won many awards for her work, including the C. L. A. Young Adult Book Award, first prize for adult fiction in the CBC Literary Competition, the Halifax Mayor's Award for Cultural Achievement in Literature, and the Order of Canada.